LANDMARKS

Black Historic Sites on the Eastern Shore of Virginia

LANDMARKS
Black Historic Sites on the Eastern Shore of Virginia

Project Committee

    Frances Bibbins Latimer
    Brenda E. Holden
    John Verrill
    Brooks Miles Barnes
    Barbara G. Cox
    George A. Latimer

Eastern Shore Center for Black History and Culture

    Frances Bibbins Latimer
    Brenda E. Holden
    Roni Lynn Jolley
    Taina Shand

Publication of this book was made possible by a grant from the Virginia Foundation for the Humanities

Published by
Hickory House
P. O. Box 37
Eastville, Virginia 23347

Library of Congress Number 2006939639

ISBN   1-886706-72-7

Printed in the United States of America
on acid-free paper.

The American Negro must remake his past in order to make his future...History must restore what slavery took away...The Negro has been a man without a history because he has been consisdered a man without a worthy culture...But already the negro sees himself against a reclaimed background, in a perspective that will give pride and self respect ample scope, and make history yield for him the same values that the treasured past of any people afford.

"The Negro Digs Up the Past"
Arthur Alfonso Schomberg

Contents

Acknowledgment

The publication of *Landmarks, Black Historic Sites on the Eastern Shore of Virginia* involved the invaluable assistance and cooperation of many people.

I was supported by The Eastern Shore Center for Black History and Culture, those individuals who feel that the history of African Americans on the Eastern Shore is important and that this book was a worthy project, lent their names and time to forming a group to encourage the research and publishing of *Landmarks*.

The Virginia Foundation for the Humanities, whose vision of documenting and interpreting African American history has made many dreams come to life all over the state of Virginia, funded this publication. Through the eyes of David Bearinger, Grant Director, the VFH was able to visualize the completion of *Landmarks* and gave their support.

Each member of the *Landmarks* Project Committee brought to this book their own special gifts and worked to design, proofread, encourage, and suggest. All of these members share with me their love of history and their determination to present the history of black people of the Eastern Shore in a truthful light.

Each historic site was plotted using Global Positioning System (GPS). This system allows permanent access to historic locations in the event that physical structures no longer exist. The need for maps using this technology brought help from several unexpected sources. A grant from RC&D, under the direction of Marian Huber, provided funding for maps. BM1 David Dickinson and BM2 Mathew Hux of Coast Guard Station Cape Charles, both familiar with GPS instruments, used their knowledge to facilitate accurate collection of map coordinates. Finally, Bill and Colette Nelson, local cartagraphers, completed these maps.

Few historical research projects could be completed on the Eastern Shore of Virginia without the help of the Clerk's Offices in Accomack and Northampton counties. These keepers of our records worked deligently to find deeds and wills and offered suggestions on where each piece of information may be stored. In addition to the Northampton County Clerk and staff, Claudia Turner Bagwell was never too busy to provide her own expertise in deed searches.

Finally, I must pay tribute to the many local individuals who were willing to share with me memories of old times, memories that they held within their hearts. They are the soul of this book.

Frances Bibbins
Eastville, Virginia 23347
October 29, 2006

x

Preface

Landmarks: Black Historic Sites on the Eastern Shore of Virginia is itself a landmark of Eastern Shore historiography. As the first work devoted exclusively to black historic sites in Accomack and Northampton counties, it examines the mostly neglected history of black institutions – churches, schools, lodges, and businesses – and the buildings that housed them.

In the years following Emancipation, black people were both pushed and pulled away from the dominant white society. Pushed away by the determination of whites to maintain black subservience; pulled away by the desire of blacks to remove themselves as far as possible from white interference. Through great effort and perseverance, blacks on the Eastern Shore managed to create a world at once separate from and parallel to that of the whites.

Although similar, the institutions that blacks created – churches, schools, fraternal orders – were not mirror images of their white counterparts. Black institutions served a political function largely unknown to those of the white, and more often in the black community than in the white a single building served a variety of religious and social purposes. Indeed, the combination church-school-lodge hall was the focal point of many a black neighborhood.

During the late nineteenth and early twentieth centuries, the Eastern Shore of Virginia became one of the richest agricultural regions in the United States. Black people did not share equally with white in the prosperity but, nevertheless, share they did. The black community's growing wealth, population, and confidence found expression in the establishment of new businesses, churches, schools, and fraternal orders and in the building and re-building of the structures that housed them. The stagnant economy and declining population that devastated the Eastern Shore in the wake of the Great Depression marred the landscape of the black community as cruelly as that of the white. Everywhere stand ghostly reminders of a more prosperous past–abandoned dwellings, commercial buildings, lodge halls, and churches.

No one knows the history of the black people of the Eastern Shore of Virginia as well as Frances Latimer. The practice of black history is exceedingly difficult. The relative poverty and illiteracy of blacks and their reticence before white authority severely limit the scope and depth of customary source materials such as correspondence and government and business records. The historian must supplement the scraps found in the usual places with insights drawn from oral tradition. Frances Latimer combines long experience in both written and oral sources with a remarkable diligence and an even more remarkable intuition. The happy result of her intelligence and industry is *Landmarks*.

Brooks Miles Barnes
Onancock, Virginia
October 29, 2006

Introduction

Landmarks is a book of black historic sites. It is not a book of tourist sites. None of these sites is open for visiting except churches on Sunday. *Landmarks* does not present complete histories of organizations, but rather a record of the buildings associated with each institution.

This book is divided into five parts: Businesses, Cemeteries, Churches, Lodges, and Schools. Each of the five categories was researched within certain parameters. Only businesses organized before 1950 are included, and only those whose founders are deceased. The churches were included if the church was founded before 1900. All surviving lodge buildings were researched. Nine private cemeteries in the African-American community were included in this book. These cemeteries span the entire spectrum of the black experience on the Eastern Shore, blacks who died and were buried as slaves, free blacks owning land before slavery was over and buried on their own land, and blacks who purchased land after slavery and were buried on their land. Although the intention was to include all African-American schools, beginning in 1867, this was not possible due to the inaccessibility of school records.

The research on this book was been done from primary sources and interviews with people having knowledge of each site. Noted local authors have written timelines and histories of the Eastern Shore without ever mentioning black people or that slavery existed on the peninsula. *Myne Owne Ground*, by T. H. Breen and Stephen Innes, and *Race and Class in Colonial Virginia*, by Douglas Deal, are the only books written about black people on the Eastern Shore and these address only the colonial period. With the exception of these books, there have been no books written about African Americans on the Eastern Shore of Virginia. Many updated church histories do not include the earliest transactions of churches, and others have been revised to eliminate the mention of slavery. Most of the lodges have disbanded as older members die off and younger people are uninterested in the lodge historical functions. There are no public records of small community businesses and newspaper advertisements for these businesses are nonexistent. School research was most difficult in that neither the Northampton nor Accomack county school divisions would make records available for this type of research. After the 1920s newspapers seldom included information about black schools. Many schools have been omitted, pending further study. The public is invited to share memories, pictures, or oral history about these schools with the author.

The Civil War ended 250 years of chattel slavery for black people in the southern United States. In most instances this book begins as the Civil War ends with black people entering mainstream society as diminished citizens without benefit of education or adequate housing. *Landmarks* begins when one day black people were slaves, barred from acting on their own behalf and the next day were free, without preparation or experience, responsible for their lives and those of their children.

The Bureau of Refugees, Freedmen and Abandoned Lands, better known as the Freedmen's Bureau, was established in March 3, 1865. The Freedmen's Bureau, headed by General O. O. Howard, was to bring normalcy to areas affected by the war, but also to create human living conditions for those most affected by slavery. It had offices in Drummondtown in Accomack County and Eastville in Northampton County. Although the original plan for the Freedmen's Bureau included both black and white citizens, white people refused participation in the program, not wanting to be in contact with black people some of whom were former slaves.[1]

The Freedmen's Bureau was funded through the War Department and at the beginning had adequate resources to accomplish its mission of opening schools, providing lands for black farmers, and work for black laborers. On the Eastern Shore the Freedmen Bureau sold and rented lands which had been confiscated during the Civil War. In Northampton County two of Miers Fisher's properties were confiscated and used as hospitals, George Ker's property was confiscated and used as headquarters for the Union Army. Both Fisher and Ker had been large land and slave owners. In Accomack, in addition to farmland confiscations, the Union Army took over the St. George Episcopal Church and the Drummondtown Methodist Church. Over time, however, President Andrew Johnson, undermined the Bureau's funding by returning all lands to their pre-Civil War owners in 1866. The newly freed slaves' position deteriorated, their chance for housing ended, and their opportunity for land vanished.

Bishop Daniel Alexander Payne

Although limited funding was a setback to the Freedmen's Bureau, black people gained by having schools that would not have been sponsored or organized by any other source. The Bureau acted as an organizing agency for local black people who had saved money they had earned from their labors, formed education boards, bought land, and built their own one- and two- room schools.

The local authorities on the Eastern Shore had no desire to provide the smallest helping hand to the people who had been held in slavery generation after generation. There were no schools for black children in either county and the local authorities had no interest in providing any.

Bishop Alexander Payne observed conditions among newly freed blacks on the Eastern Shore. Excerpts from a book written by Bishop Alexander Payne are included here because, although limited in scope they provide a view of how the former slaves lived and were regarded.

> In September I traveled south ward, giving some attention to our work on the Peninsula, or Eastern Shore of Virginia, which covers a distance of forty miles. The pioneers were Rev. J. H. A. Johnson and Rev. J. H. Offer, whom I sent from the Baltimore Conference in 1866. On the arrival of the latter at Eastville, Virginia, there was not a single house of worship, and but two small societies in the region organized by Rev. J. H. A. Johnson. Elder Offer at first preached under an oak-tree, but in 1868 six houses of worship had been erected and a seventh commenced. Since then, new ones have been erected in some places and the old ones consecrated to educational purposes.
>
> The chief employment of the colored laborers there was farming, which at that time consisted of the cultivation of both Irish and sweet potatoes, and corn. Large quantities of fish were shipped to the cities of Baltimore and Philadelphia. The steamer on which I left Onancock took away at one time one thousand and twenty-nine barrels of sweet potatoes from one point. The mental and moral condition of the people was lamentable. This is the legitimate fruit of the house of bondage [slavery] from which they had so recently issued.
>
> The following spring I visited some settlements where I found the homes most miserable, with but few exceptions. We interviewed some seven or eight heads of families—all mothers; and on my putting to each the question, "Can you read the Bible?" the invariable response was "No," in every case except one. I urged every one to go to night-school, or to Sunday-school, in order that they might learn to read the word of God. The majority promised to learn. These mothers all had children. What must become of such, if their mothers are unable to train them right? And what mother can train a child in the way it should go, if she

is not a daily, prayerful reader of the Bible?[2]

African Americans also suffered from their inability to know how to read newspapers and remained ignorant of the world around them. They could not read contracts or deeds and were often cheated out of property that they had worked hard to acquire.

Most black men were not farmers; they worked as laborers on the plantations that had been their homes during slavery. Those few who were fortunate enough to farm most often were not farmers, but share croppers, who worked for a third of the crop.

Illustrations

All photographs contained in this book were taken by the author with the exception of those listed below.

SUSAN CUSTIS RILEY'S HOUSE

Many unimposing buildings stand along Eastern Shore roadways, down long lanes, set back in woods, and on edges of fields. Nature is claiming some of them for its own, leaving just enough structure to remind this generation of what came before. These buildings tell stories of African-American history on the Eastern Shore of Virginia, stories of slavery, the struggles after slavery, and times when blacks had supposedly achieved equality.

Susan Riley's House

Few houses can be identified as slave homes, hence the importance of this one. The home's occupant, Susan Custis Riley, cannot be remembered for starting a business, building a church, preaching a sermon, or teaching a lesson. She was a slave, the daughter of parents unable to marry because they were also slaves and were not allowed to marry. Susan Custis Riley was a wife, a mother, a grandmother, a churchworker and the ancestor of many of today's Accomack County citizens.[3]

Susan Custis Riley's house is losing its battle with time. Located in Bayside on Bayside Road, this house is an important reminder of a large part of black history in the United States, a reminder of where black people started their history in this country. Susan Riley was owned by William Samuel Custis, son of Jack Custis, who lived at Deep Creek. She was born on court night and named for Peter Bowdoin's wife, Susan, who died that day. As a slave, Susan worked in the kitchen, served the table, and sewed Confederate uniforms for the Custis sons, William, John, Edward, and James, who served in the Civil War.[4]

Susan, who married Henry A. Riley in 1894, was mother of five children. She died in 1945 at the age of 102.[5]

1 *Businesses*

Before the Civil War, black people owned no businesses. Most of them lived within the confines of chattel slavery. A very few free black men were farmers, but black sawyers and firemen worked for white-owned saw mills, black watermen worked on white-owned boats, black teamsters guided white-owned wagons.

The United States Census of 1870, the first census that counted all citizens, including former slaves, lists new black occupations. Carpenters, bricklayers, cooks, and others once caught in the claws of slavery now freely plied their trade for money. Services once provided through slavery for free were now services provided for wages, small wages, but wages just the same.

When the Civil War ended, black-owned businesses began to appear in the form of cook shops, barber shops, funeral homes, and neighborhood stores. Not until the turn of the century after slavery did African-American businesses grow larger, better organized, and incorporated.

Black business owners catered to the needs of black people; black businesses were always black businesses. Black funeral directors buried black people, but never white. White undertakers on the other hand buried both black and white. Black doctors treated black patients, white doctors treated both black and white. Black preachers married black couples, white preachers married both. White people always had entry into the black world, but the opposite was not the case. Circumstances alone created two separate and very unequal worlds, which existed for generations side by side—white and black water fountains, white and black schools, and white and black beaches.

Businesses included in this book by no means represent all of the black enterprises organized on the Eastern Shore of Virginia. Indeed many hundreds of African-

American businesses are known to have operated between the Civil War and the present day. Here we have but a sample of those that have survived or that have left us sufficient representation in records or clues in cultural memory for us to tell their story. Little is known about black businesses prior to the twentieth century. For example, we know that Samuel L. Burton, Major J. Parker, Benjamin T. Coard, Henry A. Wise, and Jesse Ames set up the merchandise firm of Burton, Parker and Co. in Onancock in the late 1800s, but we don't know more, not even the nature of their merchandise.[6]

Sometimes we know the struggles, successes, or circumstances of black businesses by virtue of a news account, a line in a courthouse record, or a memory passed to us through oral history. Often, however, we don't have an exact location, owner, business type, or date. These we do not include in this book, but hope one day to learn more for another edition. Readers with information on these businesses are encouraged to contact Hickory House, so that the stories will not be lost forever. Here we list some examples of history that has survived.

Moses Simpkins owned a pool hall with a sideline business selling ice cream. When, in 1921, the town of Accomack caught fire, the fire fighters became overcome with heat. They cooled themselves by eating Simpkins' ice cream as the store burned. Simpkins, seemingly undaunted by the loss, opened another business on Church Road in Accomac.[7]

In Northampton County, Downing Beach offered free bay-front swimming to black people and a club house that hosted bands for dancing. Langston Brickhouse was the owner and proprietor of the Brickhouse Cleaners in Hare Valley. Located in Nassawadox was Francis New and Used Cars owned by Gilmore T. Francis.

Although neither site nor structure has been associated with the Northampton Land and Development Company, its historical presence may be seen in the Treherneville community. In 1901 Leonard Treherne, William H. Stevens, James C. Wyatt, Joseph F. Church, and A. T. Treherne formed a board of directors to operate this company to buy, sell, and improve land anywhere in Northampton and Accomack counties or any place in Virginia. Other members of the board were W. H. Brickhouse, Henry James, Samuel Mapp, Henry Fitchett, Jesse Fuller, Henry Addison, and John More.[8]

In 1903 the Cheapside Mercantile and Industrial Association, Inc., formed to operate a general wholesale and retail mercantile business that also conducted land cultivation for trading and bartering in farm products. The board of directors included William Banks, Arthur Banks, John O. Morris, John W. Ames, George Spady, Allen T. Ames, Major Goffigon, George M. Stevens, William Knight, and Edward Trower.[9]

The black business community included many beauty parlors, grocery stores, barber shops, cook shops, garages, gas stations, building contractors, and taxi services. Although fertile with ideas, at the turn of the century black people were but thirty-six years past slavery and underfunded. Local banks were pleased to open checking and savings accounts for their black clientele, but seldom willing to give them loans to open businesses or buy houses, seeing them as uncreditworthy.

Black businesses were not well promoted or advertised. Promotion was done by word of mouth, ads in church souvenir booklets, county fair souvenir booklets, and maybe a business card. A survey of the local newspapers from 1900 to 1950 indicates yearly advertisements for Tasley Fair and after 1926 a yearly advertisement for both the Tasley and Weirwood fairs. But no other ads were found that promoted black enterprises. As a result, one source that may be valuable for other people or other places, is not available to help record the history of black businesses on the Eastern Shore of Virginia.

AMES FUNERAL HOME, MELFA

Ames Funeral Home, located in Melfa on Route 13, was established by Alfred "Allie" Ames. He never attended school for mortuary science, nor did he hold a license to embalm. He was apprentice to Nehemiah "Nim" Saunders, which status allowed him to direct funerals. As was common for the time, Reuben Somers, Benjamin Gunter, and other undertakers were licensed only to direct funerals, not to embalm. Edgar Wharton of Wharton Funeral Home embalmed for Ames.[10]

Ames Funeral Home on Route 13

THE BRICKHOUSE BANKING COMPANY, HARE VALLEY

A Certificate of Incorporation was issued to the Brickhouse Banking Company in 1910. The principal place of business was in Hare Valley in Northampton County. The bank was formed to conduct general banking business. By law the capital stock of the bank was not to be less than $10,000.00 and not to exceed $50,000.00, divided in shares at a value of $5.00.[11]

Melvin J. Chisum, a stock speculator born in Texas but living in Norfolk, helped organize the bank and served as its first president. The other bank officers were:

Brickhouse Banking Family

Brickhouse dwelling today

Reuben B. Upshur of Hare Valley, Vice President; Jacob H. Griffith of Eastville, second Vice President; Charles J. Brickhouse of Hare Valley, Secretary; and Taylor D. Jefferson of Cape Charles, Treasurer. Other bank directors were: William H. Brickhouse and Peter Bivins, both of Hare Valley and B. T. Coard of Accomack Court House. In 1911, William H. and Janie Brickhouse deeded four acres of land for the bank's use. The Brickhouse Banking Company served the African-American community until 1916.[12] Later the brick bank building was used as a dwelling. As years went on it fell into disrepair and no longer exists.

The Brickhouse dwelling pictured here was still a part of the Hare Valley community until it burned. The charred structure still stands.[13]

CARVER MOVIE HOUSE AND THE CARVER SPOT, CAPE CHARLES

W. H. Tabb

In March of 1940 the Cape Charles Theatre Corporation was formed with three trustees, William H. Tabb, William Carrow, and W. A. Dickinson.[14] A week later the Corporation purchased two lots on the southside of Jefferson Avenue in the African-American section of Cape Charles from W. A. and Naomi Dickinson.

The primary goal of the Cape Charles Theatre Corporation was to open a movie house for black people in Cape Charles. This would become the only movie theater for blacks in all of lower Northampton County. Built of cinder blocks, the theater had a seating capacity of 400.[15] When the corporation held a contest to determine the theater's name, Bessie Trower of lower Northampton County won by suggesting "Carver" in honor of George Washington Carver, a noted black scientist of the Tuskeegee Institute in Alabama. The Carver opened on Saturday, May 24, 1940.[16]

Seven years later the Carver Spot, a soda fountain/restaurant opened on a lot adjoining the theatre. The building, also constructed of cinder block, measured 36 feet square.[17] Both buildings have been demolished.

Floyd's Restaurant, Melfa

Before the first Floyd's Restaurant could open in 1945 in the town of Melfa, arsonists burned it to the ground. The Floyd family spent two years reorganizing and building a restaurant in a different location, one mile south of the town. The new cinder block building, located on Route 13, was a family restaurant that had gas pumps and welcomed truckers. More than just a place to eat, Floyd's Restaurant sponsored a baseball team and yearly sponsored a traveling Indian show for the black community.[18]

Fernon Floyd

Fernon Floyd, the restaurant's founder, died in 1948 at age 28, just a year after the successful opening of his business.

Floyd's Restuarant continued as a family business under the leadership of Milton Floyd Senior and Milton Floyd Junior until 1967, when the widening of Route 13 forced it to close. Also situated on the Floyd property were Elsie Dennis's Beauty Parlor and Cliff Beach's Barber Shop.[19]

Floyd's Restaurant on Route 13, south of Melfa, Virginia

Gray's Funeral Home, Cape Charles

Mills Gray

In the 1880s, Mills C. Gray traveled from Nansemond County, Virginia, to Cape Charles in Northampton County. Gray established himself as a carpenter and built many of the early houses in Cape Charles, several of which still stand. A friendship between Gray and Conrad Grimmer, also a carpenter and mortician, helped Gray launch his mortuary business. Gray married Jenny Joynes, the daughter of John and Margaret Joynes. Their family included one son, Merritt Gray.

Gray's Funeral Home, founded in 1895, the first funeral home owned and operated by an African American on the Eastern Shore of Virginia, conducted business in a house built by Mills Gray at 643 Randolph Avenue. In the back yard still stands the building used for embalming and preparing the dead for burial. Thomas L. Godwin, also of Cape Charles, supplied Gray with cement burial vaults.[20]

Mills Gray died in 1934. Gray's Funeral Home was subsequently operated by his wife, Jenny, with the aid of her niece, Alston Joynes Godwin, the wife of Thomas L. Godwin. Jenny Joynes Gray died in 1946, leaving the business to niece Alston

The first Gray's Funeral Home

Gray's Funeral Home on Jefferson Avenue, Cape Charles

Godwin. The funeral home was moved after the death of Jenny Gray to Madison Avenue where the business continues in the hands of the Godwin family. Alston Godwin has retired, leaving her son, Thomas G. Godwin, and his wife, Juanita Brickhouse Godwin, in charge of this old Eastern Shore institution.[21]

GUNTER FUNERAL HOME, ONANCOCK

Benjamin F. Gunter was born in Accomack County in 1889. After beginning his life's work as a farmer and merchant in Bayside, Gunter moved to Onancock and, in partnership with his wife, Cinthia Wise Gunter, established the Gunter Funeral Home in 1931.

Although Gunter held a license to direct a funeral business and funerals, he was never a licensed embalmer and depended on Frank B. Holland of Holland's Funeral Home in Cheriton to do this work for him. When the Holland's Funeral Home expanded north to Hare Valley, Gunter reciprocated by having his daughter, Greta Taylor, direct funeral services for Holland. After

Benjamin F. Gunter

Holland's sudden death in 1958, Edgar Wharton of Wharton's Funeral Home assisted Gunter by embalming for him. Gunter died in 1970 at age 81 years. [22]

Benjamin F. Gunter stands beside a hearse

Gunter Funeral Home as it is today in Onancock, Virginia

Benjamin and Cinthia Gunter officiate at funeral

Holland's Funeral Home, Cheriton

Using land and a dwelling purchased by his parents in 1909 on Sunny Side Road, Cheriton, Frank Holland established Holland's Funeral Home in 1932.[23] In 1934 Holland married Ruby Treherne, and together they operated the business until 1935, when the funeral home was set on fire. Although the building was not destroyed, the Hollands relocated the business to Route 13 south of Cheriton.[24]

Frank Holland

Ruby Treherne Holland

As the business grew, Holland's Funeral Home began to serve more families north of Cheriton. In 1953 a second funeral home was built in Hare Valley to provide viewings and funeral services.[25]

Holland died unexpectedly in 1958, leaving the business under the direction of widow Ruby Treherne Holland until 1967, when the ownership of the funeral home

Holland Funeral Home in Hare

The first Holland's Funeral Home on Sunnyside Drive

passed to Jerome and Julia Cornish of Maryland. The name for the business was changed to Cornish-Holland Memorial Funeral Home; it is now operated by Matthew Cornish, Jr.[26]

The present Cornish-Holland Memorial Funeral Home on Business 13

JEFFERSON'S GROCERY STORE, CAPE CHARLES

In 1881, Taylor Daniel Jefferson left Nottoway County, Virginia, to make a life for himself. He went to Cape Charles in 1884, and two years later opened Jefferson's Grocery Store on Mason Avenue in partnership with his cousin. The partnership fell out when the cousin wanted to expand the business by adding spirits to its offerings. Jefferson bought out the cousin and continued serving the community as sole

Walter Jefferson, son of T. D. Jefferson, in the Jefferson's grocery store on Mason Avenue in Cape Charles.

proprietor until he died in his sleep at the age of 76 in 1936. After Jefferson's death, the store continued in operation under the management of his only son Walter Jefferson.

Jefferson's Grocery Store was not just the first black owned grocery store in Cape Charles, it was the first grocery store owned by anyone. The lot on which it stood is now vacant.[27]

THE MALLIE MOVIE HOUSE, TREHERNEVILLE

Built on land purchased by Robert Treherne, many people will recognize this site as Bob's Place and in later years as Bo-Bo's Place, two local watering holes. Originally the Mallie Theatre was a part of this complex, located on Route 13 in Treherneville to the south of the remaining decaying structures of Isaac Horton's Cleaning and Pressing Plant, a gas station, and a store.[28]

Named for Delegate Peter J. Carter's daughter, Mallie Carter Johnson, a teacher at Tidewater

Mallie Movie House

Mallie Movie House Building today

Institute, poet, and social worker, the Mallie was one of several businesses owned by the Treherne family. The youths of the 1940s tell of saving their money each week for a trip to the Mallie on Saturday night.[29]

MITCHELL'S STORE, CAPE CHARLES

Jesse Mitchell came to Cape Charles from Pottacassi, North Carolina, after 1910 and married Sallie Nottingham. During his first years there he worked for the the town as a laborer, sometimes as a drayman collecting trash with a horse and cart.[30] Jesse opened Mitchell's Store in the late 1930s and kept it open until his death when son Willis then operated it. The store is now run by the third generation of the Mitchell family, granddaughter Lenore. Neighborhood customers come and go today as they did seventy years ago, to buy a soft drink and a package of nabs and to meet and chat. Mitchell's is a Jefferson Avenue fixture.[31]

Mitchell's Store

MORRIS FUNERAL HOME AND MORRIS STORE, CHEAPSIDE AND NASSAWADOX

John Offer Morris was born in lower Northampton County in 1875. In 1898 Morris married Pauline Hodges, with whom he had five sons. In 1902 he opened a small store in Cheapside his first business venture. In 1914 Morris and Isaiah Elliott opened a mortuary in Cheapside, with Morris eventually assuming exclusive control.[32]

John O. Morris died in 1934, preceded in death by his eldest son, John O. Morris, Jr. Pauline Morris and her surviving sons kept both the store and the funeral business active and growing. The store closed after the death of Pauline Morris.

In 1954 the John O. Morris Funeral Home opened a branch in Nassawadox. Later the funeral business in Cheapside was closed. By then Alvin, the youngest Morris son, and his wife, Eunice Fisher Morris, were operating the business. In 1998,

Alvin Morris passed away. Eunice Morris, joined by her daughter, Stephanie Morris Castro, and by Eugene Bannister continue to provide a needed service to the African-American community in Northampton County.[33]

The first Morris Funeral Home in Cheapside, Virginia

The Morris Store in Cheapside Virginia

The present Morris Funeral Home in Nassawadox, Virginia

Outlaw's Blacksmith Shop, Onancock

In 1920 Samuel Outlaw left his home in North Carolina and traveled to Hampton, Virginia, to attend Hampton Normal and Agricultural Institute. There he enrolled in a four-year course in blacksmithing. Two years after graduating, Outlaw moved to Accomack County, where, at first, he lived with fellow blacksmith Matthew Hall and his family.[34]

Once he was established in the Onancock community, Outlaw purchased a house on Boundary Avenue and soon after built the 20- by 50-foot shop shown here to house his blacksmith business. From 1927, when he organized his business, until he retired in 1991, he repaired all sorts of implements of work (plows, harrows, or wheels) and implements of living (cars or bicycles).

Outlaw died in 1994 at the age of 95. His family gave the building to the Eastern Shore of Virginia Historical Society as a memorial to his life and to blacksmithing, the trade he loved and performed so well.[35]

Outlaw's Blacksmith Shop

Palm Cafe, Cape Charles

Located on the corner of Mason Avenue and Peach Street, the Palm Cafe was opened by Dutel Joynes in 1939. This full-menu restaurant catered to the African-American townspeople, north-bound travelers waiting for the train, south-bound travelers waiting for the ferry, and pullman porters and other railroad personnel.[36]

When, in 1941, Joynes was drafted into the Army, his parents Emily and Sampson Joynes and brother Oliver worked to keep the Palm Tavern open. Oliver worked part time for the railroad and part time in the restaurant.

It has been said that police officers patroled the front of the restaurant to make sure that white travelers did not enter. Palm Tavern closed in 1983 when Dutel Joynes died. Over the years the building fell into disrepair and was razed in 2003.[37]

PITTS MOVIE HOUSE, ONANCOCK

The Pitts Movie House was owned by Mary Frye Pitts, a woman known for her rich and theatrical contralto voice and for her career in teaching. After the movie business closed, this building became a night spot called the SSS Night Club.

The building now houses the New Jerusalem Holiness Church.[38]

This building formerly housed the Pitts Movie House

THE READ HOUSE, HARE VALLEY

Dr. Charles Martin Read came to the United States from Jamaica, British West Indies, in 1903. In 1912 Northampton County certified him to practice medicine in Virginia.[39] In 1916 he purchased one acre of land from James and Ann Kelley. The house built there served as his home and office.[40]

When George E. Downing, one of the Shore's first black attorneys, returned home from college to practice law, this was his office. This building also served as office space for Dr. James C. Allen in 1939 [41] and Dr. Conway Downing in 1945.[42]

The Read House

SAMPLE'S BARBER SHOP, CAPE CHARLES

Although Albert Beckett's was the first barber shop for African-American men in Cape Charles, Sample's Barber Shop is still in operation after Lloyd T. Sample opened it 104 years ago. It was first located on south Strawberry Street. When the town began to grow and white development reached southern Cape Charles, Sample was encouraged to move north, nearer to the black community.

Lloyd T. Sample

Lloyd Sample married Matilda Lanier of Southampton County, Virginia, May 25, 1903.[43] Together they had six children, two of whom, John and Paul, were active in the barbering business in Cape Charles. In the early years Russell Wilkins and Colin Morris worked as "boot blacks" in the barber shop. On the ground floor of the Strawberry Street building was a pool parlor operated by Marion Dix.

After the senior Sample died in Cape Charles, John and Paul Sample continued the business, moving it to Jefferson Avenue in the 1960s.[44] The new building was constructed on the corner of Jefferson Avenue and Straw-berry Street on the very spot that Mary Eliza Wilson had established and operated a cook shop for many years. Wilson's Cook Shop is said to have served the best "yock" ever. Sample's Barber Shop is currently operated by Willie Collins.[45]

Sample Barber Shop

SAUNDERS FUNERAL HOME, CULLS

The second oldest mortuary in Northampton County was established by John H. Saunders.[46] Saunders had been born a slave and was owned by Patsy Smith. He had worked as a carpenter during slavery. His place of business was located in Culls just down the road from where he grew up in the household of his parents, Sidney and Ibby Smith. John Saunders died in 1910 leaving his widow, Henrietta Fitchett

Saunders, and his brother, Nim Saunders, to run his business, which continued successfully for many years.

No buildings remain to mark the spot where the mortuary stood on the property once owned by John Saunders. Stories say, however, that a fire burnt down the building there called the "dead house."[47]

Tasley and Weirwood Fairgrounds

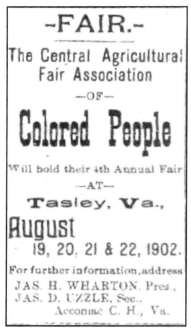

Advertisement from the Peninsula Enterprise Newspaper.

The first fair enjoyed by black people on the Eastern Shore was one sponsored by the Onawa Social Union. This fair was organized in 1891 near Mappsburg Station. The Onawa Social Union was a lodge in Accomack County. [48]

Tasley Fair, located on Tasley Fairground Road, was one of two popular summer pastimes for African Americans on the Eastern Shore of Virginia. At the end of 1800s, James H. Wharton, a local businessman, and James D. Uzzle, a public school principal, formed the Central Agricultural Fair Association. In time, other men became interested and joined as board members, including Abel S. West, Benjamin Wharton, Benjamin Coard, Dr. A. E. West, Thomas Cutler, and Levi Finney, to name just a few. In the early 1930s, Rufus Wharton, Howard Wharton, and J. Edgar Thomas, became board members. In the late 1930s, Thomas became president and manager of the Fair. Under his direction, the Central Agricultural Fair Association prospered. [49, 50]

Tasley Fairground as it looks today.

The Weirwood Fair, the other source of summer pleasure for the black community, was sponsored by the Central Northampton Agricultural Industrial Fair Association. Begun in 1926, it was located just off Bayford Road. The Fair's founding trustees were Alfonzo Fitchett, Luther Francis, Walter Jefferson, Pack Bracy Jr., Henderson Savage, Charles N. McCune, Dr. Peter Carter, C.U. Sisco, and W. C. Brown. In the later years George Smith, Sewell Harmon, George M. Smith, Willis N. Upshur. Langdon C. Morris, Charles Wright, George Savage, H. C. Press, John H. Smith, James Giddens, W. L. Lindsay, George Treherne, and Bruce Peace became members of the board of directors. The board purchased two plots of land in Weirwood, one in 1926 and one in 1927. [51, 52]

Three of the original directors of the Weirwood Fair: Alfonzo Fitchett, Luther Francis, and Walter Jefferson.

A day at the Tasley and Weirwood Fairgrounds included harness races at the track; concessions of food and novelties; games of chance at pitching pennies and knocking down pins for a prize; carnival rides of swings, the merry-go-round, the ferris wheel; and the agricultural/industrial exhibits. At end of the day every child's dream was to still be at the fair and awake to see beautiful fireworks illuminate the sky.

Entry off Bayford Road into old Weirwood Fair Ground

Winner of the day stands in front of the Grand Stand. On the first floor of the grand stand was an exhibit area for competition in canning and handcrafted items.

THOMAS FUNERAL HOME, TASLEY

Born in Baltimore, Maryland, J. Edgar Thomas moved to Accomack County in 1919. He attended Eckels School of Mortuary Science and may have been the second licensed embalmer in Northampton and Accomack counties. He worked as an apprentice under Mills C. Gray of Gray's Funeral Home in Cape Charles. He opened the first Thomas's Funeral Home in 1926 on Wharton Road. The funeral home pictured here was built and open for business in 1932 on what is now Edgar Thomas Road. He died February 7, 1961.[54, 55]

J. Edgar Thomas

Thomas Funeral Home, built in 1932

TRENT GROCERY STORE, WHITESVILLE

The Trent family has had a presence in Whitesville since Thomas and Mollie Trent came there as a young married couple. Thomas, a cooper, and Mollie, a laundress, were the parents of Bertie, Margaret, Edward, Bessie, and Herbert. Son Edward, also a cooper in a Parksley barrel factory, continued to live in Whitesville and married Undine, a teacher from Portsmouth, Virginia. Early on Edward saw a need for a grocery store in his neighborhood, and with his wife as a partner and his children as help, he opened the Trent Grocery Store in the 1940s.[56]

Trent Grocery Store in Whitesville located on Parks Street

IVAN UPSHUR'S BLACKSMITH SHOP, NASSAWADOX

Ivan Upshur of Franktown attended Hampton Normal School to learn the trades of blacksmithing and wheelwrighting. His shop was located across the railroad track on the northeast corner of Route 13 and Franktown Road. The building is no longer there.[57]

Upshur Merchants, Nassawadox

Beginning with Reuben B. Upshur, several generations of the Upshur family spent their years as merchants. Reuben Upshur's grocery store on the Bayside Road in Hare Valley served that community for many years. Sons Milton, James, and Curtis apprenticed as merchants in their father Reuben's store and then ventured out on their own.

Milton A. and Martha Upshur in front of their service station in 1927

Upshur service station in the 1950s

In 1929 Milton A. Upshur with his wife, Martha, as his partner opened a service station on Route 13 at Franktown Road. Later, the Upshur brother James opened a grocery store next to the service station and store.

Several years later and a mile north on Route 13, another Upshur brother, Curtis opened his grocery store. His wife, Selma, a beautician, established a beauty parlor in the same building.[58]

Remodeled, and still standing, north of Nassawadox

Wharton Building, Accomac

This building, once owned by Rupert Wharton, sits on land that was a part of a twenty-one acre parcel called Rural Hill. Seven acres of Rural Hill had been purchased by Rupert's father, James Wharton.[59] It is not known when the building was erected.

The building housed a general store and a pool parlor. It was the scene of enjoyment for many customers, as well as one of many quarrels and disagreements. At least one encounter ended in a death over two pennies. The perpetrator ran and was never apprehended. Some years later, another death occurred when a preacher's son became enraged and killed a patron. The business closed around 1980; its owner died in 1990. The building has been vacant since, but is still owned by members of the Wharton family.[60]

Wharton Building

Wright's Blacksmith Shop, Eastville

Almost obscured by overgrowth and time, the Wright Blacksmith Shop is barely visible on Old Town Neck Road. A graduate of Hampton Institute, William Temple Wright of Walkerton, Virginia, moved to the Eastern Shore in 1916. More than just a place of business, the shop is remembered in the neighborhood as a place where men gathered to play checkers, dominoes, and pass the time of day. The business continued into the 1950s, when farming became mechanized and the need for blacksmiths diminished. Later in in his career, William Wright became a farrier and devoted his life to tending to race horses.[61]

Blacksmith Wright at work

W. T. Wright   Blacksmith Shop

2 Cemeteries

When slaves died, they were usually wrapped in a sheet and buried on the property of their owner. Free blacks were buried on the plantation on which they worked or at the Alms House in Machipongo or Parksley. Before 1831, black people who had sought refuge and lived in Indian Town were buried there. A final resting place was a worry for each free person.

After slavery had ended, the newly organized black churches took on the responsibility of burying church members. Most church by-laws included cemetery space for "members in good standing," that is, dues-paying members. As African Americans began to purchase land, many staked off a plot for burying family and friends. Many of these cemeteries were lost as the older generations died and properties changed hands. Cemeteries lie untended near roadsides and in corners of yards, the dead unknown today except for the name that appears on the gravestone. Coffin-size depressions in the earth are all that mark many burial places, unidentified and untended.

The earliest known black family cemetery in Northampton County is to be found on the land of Samuel Bibbins, land he purchased in 1851. Buried in that cemetery are family members, friends, and farm workers. The age of the Bibbins grave yard, however, does not rival that of Accomack County's Guinea Cemetery near Pungoteague, which dates to the end of the 1700s.

Various individual graves and sites with but two or three people lie in the fields of the Eastern Shore. Peter and Mary Susan Bailey, presumably husband and wife, both born in 1837, lie in a field near Middlesex in Accomack County. Rike and Margaret Stephens, also born in the 1830s, rest in a tiny over-grown fenced-in area near Onley. Delaware Kellam, his wife Kitty, and their daughter lie in a field Kellam once owned on Cobb Station Road in Northampton County. The Kellam stones are cracked and scarred by farmers claiming the family's final resting place for more land to farm.

Bailey Cemetery, Melfa

Moses Bailey was born a slave in 1854. He purchased the property called "the Nancy Nelson Land" in 1906 from the Bagwell C. Mears estate. In 1923 he purchased two more acres from William H. and Hennie A. Hickman.[62] Bailey lived in the house to the west of the cemetery and farmed the land all around it until his death in 1939. His wife, Ann, and several of his children, grandchildren, and great-grandchildren are also buried here. His youngest child, Lucy Smith, spoke often of Daddy Moses and of her pride in keeping the cemetery.[63] She minded the cemetery until her death at age 98 in 2005. Aunt Lucy is also buried here.

Moses Bailey Cemetery

Bibbins Cemetery, Eastville

The Samuel Bibbins Cemetery is probably the oldest known African-American cemetery in Northampton County. Bibbins purchased the property from George W. Brittingham in 1851.[64] The first recorded burial in the cemetery occurred in 1867 when Sam Bibbins, a namesake nephew of the owner, died of pneumonia. The last person to be buried here was Littleton Robert Bibbins, a son of the original owner, who was laid to rest in 1927. The cemetery covers an acre and contains many graves. It is located near the end of Captain Howe Drive, south of Eastville.[65]

Tomb of Emma Scisco Bibbins

BRICKHOUSE CEMETERY, HARE VALLEY

William H. and Janie Brickhouse owned land that stretched from the Bayside Road to what is now Route 13. [66] On that land was a house, a bank, a store, and this cemetery. Many members of the Brickhouse family are buried here, beginning with William H. and Janie Brickhouse.[67] This cemetery is still active.

Brickhouse Cemetery

BURRIS GRAVEYARD AND HOME, EASTVILLE

Burris Home and Cemetery

The Burris Cemetery lies behind the Burris house. Many years ago, this area was called Burristown.[68] The house was built in the 1860s by Reverend Caleb James Burris, the first black ordained minister on the Eastern Shore of Virginia. He was the founder of the Union Baptist Church. At one time Burristown consisted of three Burris houses Jacob and Anna Burris Griffith, daughter of Caleb and Eugenia, lived in a yellow house on the corner of Route 13 and Kendall Grove Road, now called Cherry Dale; and two additional houses were occupied by Caleb Burris and his son, George.

The cemetery is small and contains the burial places for Caleb Burris, his wife Eugenia, several of their children, and one son-in-law. Most of the property remains in the hands of the Burris family. The last person to live in the house was Jack Burris, the great-grandson of Caleb and Eugenia Burris, who died in 1999.[69]

The Carter Cemetery, Franktown

The Carter Cemetery is the final resting place of the Honorable Peter J. Carter, the only African American from the Eastern Shore elected to the Virginia legislature. The cemetery is located on the Bayside Road south of Franktown, near the site of the Carter family home, which burned some years ago.[70] Among those buried in the cemetery are Peter Carter's mother Peggy, his first wife Georgiana Mapp Carter, his

Gravestone of
Hon. Peter J. Carter

Carter Cemetery

second wife, Maggie Treherne Carter, and several of his children including a son, Dr. Peter J. Carter. Nim Saunders, the second husband of Maggie T. Carter, and their son, John A. Saunders are also buried in this cemetery[71]

Guinea Graveyard, Boston

In 1806 white slave owner Abel West freed all of his slaves by deed. In his 1816 will, West left to these freed slaves two hundred acres. The land was given to them and their heirs to live on forever as a place of refuge. They also received "30 barrels of corn & 1,100 weight of pork, all the flax, wool & leather that may be in the house at my death."

There was most likely that a slave graveyard was on this property, as there is now a cemetery there named Guinea. It is also likely that the slaves owned by West were imported from Guinea. Guinea Cemetery in Boston is probably the oldest known black cemetery on the Eastern Shore of Virginia. The slaves freed by Abel West included the following: Adam West, born about 1790, Annis West, born about 1800, Billy West, born about 1787, Bridget West, born about 1778, Fanny West, born about 1803, Frank West, born about 1789, Genny, born about 1785, James West, born about 1801, Mary West, born about 1788, Nancy, born about 1770, Parker West, born March 20, 1795, Saul West, born about 1790, Stran West, born June 1793, and Zipper West, born about 1800. It seems reasonable that these people were buried in this cemetery. Guinea Cemetery lies between Boston and Craddockville.[72]

JOHNSON-AYRES CEMETERY, WARDTOWN

The names on the graves found in Johnson-Ayres Cemetery in Wardtown tell the genealogy of this family. Located behind the house of the late John "Will" Ayres and

Johnson/Ayers Cemetery

Emma Johnson Ayres, the land was originally owned by Amanda Francis Johnson and Jefferson Johnson.[73] Until recently the house was occupied by the twin daughters of John and Emma Johnson Ayres. The Johnson-Ayres Cemetery is still in use in Wardtown.[74]

THE MAPP CEMETERY, MAPPSVILLE

The Mapp Cemetery is on the Mapp Farm purchased by Vianna Wescott from Leonard Nottingham and his wife Emeline in 1876.[75] The cemetery remains in the hands of Wescott descendants, now the Mapp family. It contains five known graves: those of the three sisters Laura Carpenter (died in 1919), Vianna Wescott (died 1906), and Comfort Mapp, and that of Matthew Carpenter who died in 1915, the husband of Laura. The fifth grave holds the remains the six year old grandson of Vianna, who died of lockjaw at the turn of the century.[76]

Vianna Wescott Stone

SAUNDERS/BAKER CEMETERY

The Saunders/Baker Cemetery is located in Culls in the yard of property once owned by Sidney "City" Saunders, progenitor of the Saunders/Baker family.

Sidney Saunders Cemetery

Born a slave and owned by the Saunders family at Tower Hill, Sidney "City" Saunders married Ibby Smith, a slave of Patsy Smith Widgeon. The Saunders family acquired the land from Saunders' wife's former owner as payment to settle a debt incurred by the Smith's brother. The brother had an alchohol habit and over the years of freedom Sidney Saunders had loaned him money. When approached by Saunders for repayment of his money, the brother said "go to my sister, she'll take care of it." When he went to her she said that she had no money and City should lay off land in what he thought would repay him. The deed for the land is dated 1876 in the amount presumably owed to Saunders of $100.00. This became the Saunders/Baker homestead.[77]

City Saunders is buried in the cemetery beside Ibby his wife of many years and other Baker, Saunders, and Belmond family members. The cemetery is still active.[78]

3 Churches

Africans did not come to the new world without a tradition of religious worship. Early in this history, arriving people who did not embrace Christianity were not accorded the same rights as those who were or became Christians. In many cases Christianity was used as a litmus test, and those who were not Christian became slaves as black codes grew to close off the Africans from freedom

An Act of the Virginia General Assembly passed in 1831 mandated that no one could preach to slaves nor could slaves listen to preaching unless accompanied by their owner. The law, passed after the Nat Turner Insurrection, was intended reduce the incidents of slave insurrection on the Eastern Shore.

For many years, slave owners were required to take their slaves to church with them. Even after slavery had ended, white church officials tried to maintain control by enforcing this requirement. In some churches slave entrances were constructed so

The slave door at Holmes Presbyterian Church, once used for slaves to enter and climb the stairs to the balcony of the church, is now closed.

that they could enter the church separately from the white members and be seated in a segregated area. Some of the slave entrances led upstairs into balconies. Holmes Presbyterian Church in Bayview is an example. Other churches provided only outdoor space for slaves.

Churches kept lists of the slaves who were required to attend services. Oral history tells us that the "religious" message most frequently conveyed to slaves in attendance was "Slave, obey your master." The not uncommon notion that slaves were welcomed as equals in established white churches is a faulty one that lessens the perceived severity of slavery and softens the view of the condition of black people during slavery.

When slavery ended, one of the first institutions to emerge within the black community was the church. A Freedmen's Bureau report states that freedmen seemed to be more interested in building churches than they were in building schools.

Black Baptist and African Methodist Episcopal churches developed almost simultaneously. Black Baptist churches were organized by local ministers, many of whom had been slaves on the Eastern Shore. These churches grew more easily and quickly because the Baptist church had no central head. Each church was an autonomous body. Any group of people with the desire to become a church could organize themselves to be a Baptist church.

Most of the early A. M. E. churches on the Eastern Shore were organized by Reverend John H. Offer during his two terms of office as pastor at the Bethel African Methodist Episcopal Church in Eastville. Other black Methodist churches resulted from the work of white northern missionaries and the Delaware Methodist Conference. Most of these churches are now United Methodist churches..

ADAMS UNITED METHODIST CHURCH, WHITESVILLE

Adams United Methodist Church, located at the intersection of Church Street and Leemont Road, was born in 1878 when some members of Johnson Metropolitan Methodist Church found it more convenient to worship close to home. They secured

Adams United Methodist Church

the use of a hall and began meeting in what became Whitesville. During good weather they gathered outside. On occasion they would put up a tent and have service there.

The church building was erected during the administration of Reverend J. K. Adams. The church became Adams Methodist Church of the Leemont Charge. Among the founding members were James Parks, Samuel J. Horsey, Smith Clayton, George Wright, and Wilson James.[79]

In 1897, the trustees of the Johnson Metropolitan Methodist Church and Adams Methodist Church purchased land from L. James Gunter for a parsonage in Wiseville near the old Ayres Methodist Church.[80]

In 1928, Adams Methodist Church was badly in need of renovation. Refurbishing commenced under the administration of Reverend R. C. Hughes, the sixth pastor. Alonzo Brown a carpenter from Crisfield, Maryland, rebuilt the church.

Under the leadership of Reverend A. L. Scribner, the tenth pastor, new furniture was purchased for the sanctuary and the basement was made livable.

Although renovated, Adams United Methodist Church retains its original structure.

AFRICAN BAPTIST CHURCH, CHERITON

A few members of the Union Baptist Church in Eastville who lived nearer to Cheriton met and organized the African Baptist Church. Among its founders were Reverend Alfred Spady, Ben Evans, Arthur Goffigon, Robert Wilkins, and Mary Spady.[81]

Each Sunday, the group assembled for worship at various designated locations until it became strong enough to secure a special meeting place. Toward the end of the 1860s, under the leadership of Reverend Caleb Burris, African Baptist Church began to make plans to build a house of worship.

African Baptist Church in 1947

In 1869 church trustees Arthur Goffigon, Robert Henry, Lighty Solomon, Robert Wilkins, and Nimrod Collins purchased an acre of land from William W. and Margaret Andrews located on what is now Sunny Side Drive toward the Seaside of Northampton County near Oyster.

Twenty-two years later, African Baptist Church's membership had outgrown their church. On November 17, 1891, one half acre of land was purchased from George F. Wilkins on Sunny Side Road several miles west of the original church. Church trustees Nim Saunders and Henry Baker, both members of African Baptist Church and carpenters, were

African Baptist Church as it appears today

employed to build a larger church. The old cemetery near the village of Oyster reveals grave markers of the original church site.[82]

Union Baptist Church shared its first three pastors, Reverends Caleb Burris, William H. Corbin, and Isaac Lee, with African Baptist Church. When Union Baptist Church decided to hold services weekly, Reverend Lee resigned, and African Baptist Church called Reverend George E. Reid, the first principal of Tidewater Institute. Reid was the first pastor not shared with Union Baptist.

In May of 1961, Reverend Charles F. Mapp was hired; he began his duties on the first Sunday in June. In 1966, under Mapp's guidance, the building improvements project began. During this time, the educational building was built, and brick veneering was added to the church. Mapp continues as the leader of African Baptist Church.[83]

African Baptist Church Parsonage

A vacant lot west of the church parsonage owned by the church was purchased by African Baptist Church. This was the site of the Mount Maria Tents #35. Aside from serving the black community as a civic organization, the Mount Maria Tents provided space for the Tidewater Institute before the school was able to build a facility.

BETHEL A.M.E. CHURCH, EASTVILLE

Bethel A. M. E. Church is the oldest African Methodist Episcopal church in Northampton County. Preparations for the church began shortly after the Civil War, when Bishop Daniel Payne sent Reverend James H. A. Johnson of Baltimore to the Eastern Shore of Virginia.

Johnson, the first African Methodist Episcopal missionary to minister to the spiritual needs of the newly freed black population, arrived at Cherrystone on December 20, 1865. He wasted no time in beginning his work among the black people of the Eastern Shore. The first meeting of African Methodism was held that December evening, about one half mile from Eastville. The meeting was well attended. Forty people enrolled their names for organization and membership of this new church. The group was racially mixed: black people, who came to join the new church; white people, who came to observe; and Union soldiers, who came as peace keepers. We can imagine a serious deliberation with Johnson, but no church was organized at the first meeting.[84]

Johnson went to Accomack County on January 6, 1866. There he organized Macedonia A. M. E. Church in Drummondtown, the first A. M. E. Church in Accomack County. He returned to Eastville the next day, January 7, 1866, to organize

Bishop Alexander Wayman

John H. Offer

an African Methodist Episcopal church in that town. The meeting, held at Deep Branch in an American Missionary Society school, near Eastville, resulted in formation of the first African Methodist Episcopal Church in Northampton County, called Wayman's Chapel, named for Reverend Alexander W. Wayman, an African Methodist bishop. About two weeks later, on January 22, 1866, the first quarterly conference was held in Eastville. Wayman's Chapel drew its membership from the newly freed slaves of surrounding plantations: Hesse Castle, Selma, Kendall Grove, Cessford, and Westover, as well as from already free black people with leanings toward Methodism.

In three months, Johnson had served as facilitator and overseer of the founding of three African Methodist Episcopal churches on the Eastern Shore. In spring of 1866, having accomplished all that was expected of him, and having met his own goals, Johnson went to Washington, D. C., where, on April 10, he reported to the annual conference. At this meeting, Reverend John H. Offer received his first assignment in the Methodist Church as the first pastor of Wayman's Chapel.

Born a free man in Anne Arundel County, Maryland, in February 1825, John Henry Offer married Martha Ellen Parker in Baltimore in 1853. Eleven years later he joined the army to fight for freedom for slaves. Offer served as a sergeant in Company H of the 30th Regiment of Colored Infantry during the Civil War. Before his tenure as pastor in Eastville was complete, Offer had organized Ebenezer A. M. E. in Capeville, New Allen Memorial A. M. E. in Franktown, Shorter's Chapel A. M. E. in Bridgetown, Saint Paul's A. M. E. in Pungoteague, Saint Joseph A. M. E. in Belle Haven, and Mount Zion A.M.E. in Jamesville. Offer worked unceasingly to spread the word of God and convert black people to the Methodist religion.

In 1868 the trustees of Wayman's Chapel, Andrew J. Fry, James Brown, Isaac

Brown, George Jones, and Samuel Baker, purchased one acre of land just north of Eastville from Severn and Margaret Eyre. On that land, Offer constructed the first building dedicated for worship by the congregation of Wayman's Chapel. He secured lumber from the western shore, had it shipped from Baltimore to Hungars Landing in Old Town Neck and then transported to Eastville by horse and cart. The new building, sufficient for use by a new congregation, was a single room built between the present sites of the church and the parsonage. A parsonage was also built to house Offer and his family. The claims on Offer's time grew to be so great that he was able to preach at services only once a month.[85]

After his five-year tenure on the Eastern Shore, Offer was replaced by Reverend Aaron Pindle in 1871. In 1872 the congregation voted Pindle out, and Offer returned to Bethel to serve until 1875. In 1879 Pindle was expelled from the Virginia Conference for "immoral conduct."

Reverend Robert Davis came to Bethel in 1878. During his tenure it became obvious that Wayman's Chapel had outgrown the one room church built during Offer's time. A new church was built that could accommodate 300 to 400 people. Davis served Bethel until 1882.

Reverend George D. Jennerson began his tenure in 1898, and by 1903 he had built the present Bethel A. M. E. Church. During these years the membership increased rapidly.

Reverend Isaac Ewer replaced Jennerson in 1903. During his term, Ewer held fundraisers to provide pews, carpets, chandeliers, pulpit chairs, and 500 chairs for the balcony.

Reverend J. Wright began his years of leadership in 1922. During his tenure, the present parsonage was built. These years set the scene for tumultuous times later. In 1923 the church and land were mortgaged to buy land west of the road that leads to Old Town Road.

In 1940, when Reverend R. L. Upshaw was assigned to Bethel, the

Bethel A. M. E. Church

indebtedness on the church property had been lingering for years. Under the Upshaw administration, the church was unable to keep paying on its long-time debts,

Bethel A. M. E. Parsonage

and it was sold at public auction. On March 21, 1942, in front of the Eastville Inn in Eastville, Mannie Mears, wife of attorney Benjamin Mears, made the highest bid on the church and all of its property.

The dire circumstances brought Bishop Monroe Davis to the Eastern Shore to meet with church trustees James Allen, Charles McCune, Samuel Davis, Lloyd Widgeon, and Presiding Elder I. T. Walker. They met in Benjamin Mears' office. Bishop Davis offered to pay the debt and recover the property, but the trustees turned down the proposal. The members of the church worked diligently and, in April 1942, Bethel A. M. E. trustees purchased the church from Mannie Mears for $9,000.00.[86]

Over the years, under various pastors, Bethel A. M. E. Church has been covered with siding and windows have been replaced, but the most beautiful part of the church, the tongue and grove ceiling, remains intact.

BETHEL A. M. E. CHURCH, ONANCOCK

Bethel A. M. E. Church in Onancock was organized by John H. Offer in 1868. On November 30th in that year, Bethel, then known as Onancock A. M. E. Church, purchased one acre of land from Margaret Snead. Church trustees Lewis Parker, George Custis, Lewis Revell, Thomas Watson, and Jesse Major paid $200.00 for the land.[87]

In 1868 Bethel, not unlike other A. M. E. churches, sponsored an elementary school. This school was named Armstrong School after Union General Samuel Chapman Armstrong, and it met in the church in Onancock. General Armstrong worked for the Freedmen's Bureau.

As freedom changed the lives of former slaves, they found new names, they found new jobs, and they found new places to live. The black population of Onancock shifted geographically to accommodate their new lives. Bethel A. M. E. needed to move the church nearer to its congregation. By the turn of the century this was accomplished. In November 1902, Sylvester Hackett and his wife Hester sold the new church site to James Reed, Levi Conquest, William D.

Bethel A. M. E. Church, Onancock

Wise, James T. White, Douglas Read, Henry Snead, Louis Bundick, John Poulson, and Thomas Topping, trustees of the Bethel A. M. E. Church. It is now located on Boundary Street in Onancock.[88]

BETHEL BAPTIST CHURCH, FRANKTOWN

Franktown's Bethel Baptist Church was organized in 1882. Meetings having been held in the homes of several of the members for a few months, the membership decided that a church should be built. Reverend Thomas Byrd was called to lead them, and shortly thereafter the Honorable Peter J. Carter, a former black member of the General Assembly, gave land for the church to be built on. Also, John E. Nottingham, a white friend of the congregation, contributed a sum of money for the same purpose. The church was built and prospered. Byrd served until his death; his replacement was Reverend Thomas Turlington.[89]

Peter J. Carter

At the turn of the century, Maggie T. Carter, widow of Peter J. Carter, gave Bethel Baptist Church additional land for the cemetery.[90] A hundred years later Carter's grandson, Dr. Arthur T. Carter, gave the church land for the parking lot with the understanding that all church members would register to vote.[91]

Under the pastorate of Reverend L. L. Ford, the original framed church building was renovated and veneered with stone in 1957. In 1969, also under the leadership of Ford, an annex was added. Reverend Carl Baylark followed Reverend Ford and in 1986 Baylark guided the addition of a pastor's study and a classroom. Five years later, a baptismal pool was installed, and the pulpit was moved and elevated. In 1991 Baylark resigned the pastorate of Bethel Baptist Church to answer a call extended to him by a church in Rhode Island.

Bethel Baptist Church

BURTON'S CHAPEL INDEPENDENT METHODIST CHURCH, LOCUST MOUNT

According to local belief, both black and white people were taught at Oak Grove Methodist Church Sunday School, the white people during the day and the black people at night. These black people formed the Burton Chapel Methodist church

Burton Independent Methodist Church

In 1871 Burton Chapel Methodist Church trustees Samuel Burton, Isma Shields, Charles Mears, Peter Shields, and James Johnson purchased one acre from Richard W. and Susan Ames. [92]

The present church was built in 1897. According to the church history, it was not until 1897 that the congregation had grown sufficiently to merit its own pastor, and the Reverend Joshua Waters was so assigned by the Methodist conference. By 1922, continued growth of the church made it necessary to expand the church. During the Great Depression,

Burton's Chapel Methodist struggled to survive, and at Depression's end, the church was sorely in need of repair and renovation. The cement steps were added at that time. Since 1974 Burton's Chapel has used the old Burton Elementary School as a dining hall. A hall is now being added to the church.[93]

CHERRYSTONE BAPTIST CHURCH, CHERRYSTONE

In 1879, Union Baptist Church in Eastville and African Baptist Church in Cheriton, both wishing to build a Baptist church within traveling distance of all in the vicinity who wanted Baptist teachings, joined in leasing lots 144 and 146 in Cherrystone from William H. Kimberly of Fort Monroe. The lease rate of $1.00 per year was payable in advance for the term of ninety-nine years. An African-American community was planned around the church, and several lots were purchased. The community, however, failed to thrive, and the growth of the church was limited.[94]

It is not known how long the church survived, but the Eastern Shore Baptist Association held its founding meeting at that location in 1884, indicating that it must have been a viable organization for at least five years. The building lasted well into the twentieth century before falling from lack of use and attention.

CHRIST UNION BAPTIST CHURCH, CHINCOTEAGUE

Founded in 1876, Christ Union Baptist Church is one of several churches founded by Reverend James Cluff during his crusade to spread religion throughout the black community in upper Accomack County. The congregation of Christ Union Baptist Church was never large, and during almost a century of service, its membership decreased along the black population on Chincoteague. Between 1950 and 1960, it became apparent that not only had members died, but younger members were leaving Chincoteague. In the early 1960s, the decision was made to disband the few remaining members to churches on the mainland. Two couples well remembered by Jerusalem Baptist Church members as transferring from Christ Union Baptist are Welton and Carrie Parks and Clarence and Elizabeth Marshall.[95]

James Cluff

Christian Union A. M. E. Church, Modest Town

By April 9, 1866, Reverend James H. A. Johnson had already organized Macedonia A. M. E. Church in Accomac and Wayman's Chapel A. M. E. Church in Eastville. Once again Johnson went to Accomack County. There he organized the Christian Union A. M. E. Church in Modest Town with eight members. Two years later a mob of white people seeking to curtail political meetings at the church, burned the building to the ground.[96]

It took seven years for the members of the Christian Union A. M. E. to construct a second church, also in Modest Town. In 1873 trustees William Broadwater, Ephraim Teagle, Samuel Wise, Francis Lewis, and Levin W. Gaines purchased land for a burial ground from William and Mary J. Pettit.[97] It is not known how long the second church survived.

Deas Chapel Methodist Church, Horntown

In 1866 the very wealthy Daniel Nash of New York City secured for his young wife, Catharine, a property that would be named Nashville Plantation in Winder Neck near Horntown. By 1870 a group of African Americans with leanings toward the Methodist religion began holding services on this property and built a small mission there. After several years the structure burned, and this nameless group of black Methodists was left without a place of worship.[98]

In the meantime, Daniel Nash died, and Catharine married Richard M. H. Deas. In 1877, acting as trustee for Catharine Deas, Richard Deas sold one acre of

Deas Chapel

land to the unnamed religious group for $1.00. That year, a church was built on this property. This group became members of Deas Chapel Methodist Church, named for Catharine Deas, their benefactor.

Later, Catherine Deas sold the Nashville Plantation to Edward and Marietta Clarke of Pocomoke City, Maryland. In 1885, the Clarkes sold land to Deas Chapel trustees Lewis H. Douglas, Peter Logan Sr., Thomas Douglas, George Copes, and James J.

Johnson to enlarge holdings and provide space for a cemetery.[99] In 1897 the church was rebuilt. In 1915, the church purchased land from Stephen Townsend to build a parsonage.[100]

Under the leadership of Reverend Scott, each family in Deas Chapel Church purchased a stained glass window. In 1962, during the tenure of Reverend Barclay, the church was remodeled, and a dining hall and an educational building were constructed.

EBENEZER A. M. E. CHURCH, CAPEVILLE

Before the Ebenezer A. M. E. Church was organized, a group of lower Eastern Shore residents began meeting outdoors near Cheapside. At these meetings, the group had opportunity to listen to both Reverend Caleb Burris from the Union Baptist Church and Reverend John Offer, the minister at Bethel A. M. E. Church. After some time, the group decided that a church was needed. In the course of discussion, the group realized that some people wanted to built a Baptist church while others wanted to built a Methodist church.

Ebenezer A. M. E. Church

In 1875 Ebenezer A. M. E. Church trustees James Becket, Nathaniel Jarvis, Nelson Nottingham, and John Nottingham purchased 1½ acres of land for $50.00 from George and Clara Neilson of Washington, D. C., on which to build their church. Although this church is often called Capeville A. M. E. Church it is located nearer to Cheapside, Virginia.[101]

On the third Sunday in January 1938, the building was destroyed by fire. Plans were soon in motion to rebuild the church. Over the years this second religious structure has been renovated.[102]

Ebenezer A. M. E. Church Parsonage

EBENEZER BAPTIST CHURCH, WARDTOWN

The Ebenezer Baptist Church of Wardtown was organized in 1871 by Reverend Jasper Savage, a former slave who had been freed by Arthur R. Savage. Savage was at first a member of the Zion Methodist Church of Jamesville, but after visiting several Baptist Churches and joining in worship with them, Savage found their spirituality more to his liking. Savage and several members of Zion A. M. E. Church withdrew their membership and were baptized by Reverend Caleb Buriss, a Baptist preacher. This small group organized a new church, which came to be called Ebenezer Baptist Church. Savage served as their pastor. Among his first deacons were Richard Milby, John Gunter, and Spencer Savage, a brother of Jasper Savage. Among the church ladies were Ida James and Bethney Sample.

The congregation first met under an oak tree. In 1871 they built the first church. The congregation grew quickly and after a few years a new church was built. On a Thursday afternoon in 1909, Savage baptized Eliza Gray and George Johnson. This

Ebenezer Baptist Church

was Reverend Savage's last official church act. Soon thereafter, Savage's health began to fail, and he needed the help of others to attend church service. On June 13, 1909, Savage died.

Reverend Leonard Treherne of Birdsnest was called as pastor for Ebenezer Baptist Church after Savage died. Treherne, an experienced clergyman, had been the co-founder of the Eastern Shore

Early picture of Ebenezer Baptist Church

Jasper Savage Stone

Baptist Association and the founder of Antioch Baptist Church in Treherneville. Treherne was also a partner in a real estate business. He served until he was too infirm to attend service.

Ebenezer Baptist Church next called Reverend I. S. Arnold of Portsmouth, Virginia. Arnold served until 1930, when he suffered a stoke and his health no longer permitted him to serve. Reverend R. W. Wilson became the next pastor of church. Under his administration a 96 year tradition of service on one or two Sundays per month changed, and on the first Sunday in January, 1968, Ebenezer converted into a "every Sunday" church. Also, under the leadership of Reverend Wilson the church was veneered.[103]

FIRST BAPTIST CHURCH, CAPE CHARLES

One year after the founding of the town of Cape Charles and after rail service into it had begun, the Hollywood Baptist Church began with prayer meetings at houses of members. In March, 1885, a small group of people met in a rented building on Strawberry Street and organized the Hollywood Baptist Church. The first official meeting for this group was held on the dock of the N. Y. P. & N. Railroad.

The first church service was held in the rented building on Strawberry Street in the downtown section of Cape Charles. The first church building was erected on a lot given to the church by the Scott Estate. It was constructed in the 600 block of Monroe Avenue, under the supervision of Deacon H. C. Howard.

In the summer of 1885, the church called its first pastor, Reverend I. B. Randolph. In 1893, Reverend W. M. Dixon, of Hampton, Virginia, was called as pastor. Under Dixon's administration, the church's name was changed to First Baptist Church of Cape Charles, and church membership rose to 65 or more. In 1899 Reverend George E. Reid, then pastor of the African Baptist Church at Cheriton and principal at Tidewater Institute, was called as pastor and remained there for one year. During that year a lot was purchased on Madison Avenue, and the church building was removed from Monroe Avenue to the new lot. [104]

First Baptist Church during the 1920s

On May 1st, 1900, Reverend W. H. Davenport became pastor. Under Davenport, a new church building (the present church) was erected and paid for. In 1914 Reverend P. W. Cook was called as pastor. Like Reid, Cook was employed by Tidewater Institute. Born in Detroit, Michigan, Cook married Comfort Collins. Under Cook, the church membership doubled, and new pews and lights were installed along with other interior improvements. Cook resigned in 1926. [105]

On the first Sunday in April, 1958, Reverend R. W. Wilson took charge as pastor. Under his administration, the church parsonage was completely furnished, and the church building was redecorated inside and out. An education building was erected at the rear of the church.

First Baptist Church, Cape Charles, as it looks today

First Baptist Church, Capeville

During the last quarter of the nineteenth century, a group of black Christians of lower Northampton County held religious services near the village of Cheapside. If the weather was favorable, they would meet on Sunday afternoons and worship under a shade tree.

First Baptist Church, Capeville, 1920s

Reverend W. H. Offer, the Methodist minister, and Reverend Caleb Burris, the Baptist minister, preached on alternate Sundays, familiarizing the congregation with the beliefs and practices of both religions.

After this group worshiped together for some time, the need for a building became evident. When they

Old First Baptist Parsonage

First Baptist Church, Capeville

began to organize to build, there arose a division within the group: part of the congregation was partial to Methodism and wanted to build an A. M. E. church; the other part wanted to build a Baptist church. They agreed to split and two churches were born out of this devout group~the First Baptist Church of Capeville and the Ebenezer A. M. E. Church in Cheapside.

Under the leadership of Reverend John Smith, the First Baptist Church of Capeville was formed on March 27, 1876. In 1877 trustees Fountain Booker, John Williams, and John Knight purchased three acres of land from John H. Goffigon, and the first church was built. Smith served for only a short period of time and was replaced by Reverend T. W. Nettles. Nettles served the congregation of First Baptist Church for 22 years. During these years, the second church was built and a parsonage was built in Cheapside, Virginia.[106]

In 1920 Reverend J. A. Martin became the fifth pastor of First Baptist Church, Capeville. During Martin's administration, the sexton's house was purchased. It is generally believed that during the

Sexton's House

Baptist Parsonage

49

Hopeville Mission in Cedar Grove

years the sexton's house was in service, only one family, that of Robert and Florence Jones, lived there and served the church as sextons. Land was purchased next to the sexton's house to build a church parsonage. [107]

In 1934 the church called Reverend Daniel J. Black, former pastor of a church in Bowers Hill, Virginia, and of Emanuel Baptist Church, Hilton Village, Virginia. Under Black's guidance, a parsonage was built across the highway from the church, next to the sexton's house.[108]

At Black's death in 1950, Reverend C. M. Heidelberg was called. During Black's administration, the old church, which had been used for meetings and additional space, was torn down, and an annex begun. Before this project could be finished, Heidelberg resigned.[109]

A discussion of First Baptist Church of Capeville and its buildings would not be complete without mentioning Hopeville Mission. Many members of First Baptist Church were previously members of Hopeville Mission in Cedar Grove. Hopeville Mission was very small, but it was located near a well-populated black settlement. It was active in the middle 1920s, but it is not known just when it was organized and when it disbanded.

FIRST BAPTIST CHURCH, MAPPSVILLE

The First Baptist Church of Mappsville was organized in 1875. The trustees secured land on what is now Route 600 east of the hamlet of Mappsville. Reverend A. J.

First Baptist Church, Mappsville

Satchel, also pastor of Metompkin Baptist Church, was the first leader. When Reverend J. C. Collins came to the church in 1879, he found a small rudimentary building. Not until 1900 was the church remodeled. In 1929, Reverend M. T. Boone came to pastor the First Baptist Church. Under his leadership, the old church was rebuilt and the present church came into being.[110]

Friendship Methodist Church, Wattsville

Established in 1865, Friendship Methodist Church was the first Methodist church founded in Accomack County under the leadership of the Delaware Conference; it is not an A. M. E. Church. The land was purchased from George and Elizabeth Wallop for $40.00 by the church trustees Samuel Marshall, Jacob Godwin, Henry Riley, George Conner, Henry Drummond, Peter Logan, and Henry Savage.[111] The first church was built in 1868 and rebuilt in 1926. In 1986 the Friendship Community Center, named the E. Phillip Terrell Chapel, was built as an addition to the original sanctuary.[112]

Friendship Methodist Church

Gaskins Chapel A. M. E. Church, Savageville

In *My Recollections of African M. E. Ministers, or Forty Years' Experience in the African Methodist Episcopal Church*, Reverend Alexander W. Wayman recorded that on Sunday, June 12, 1870, he was called to Savageville on the Eastern Shore of Virginia to dedicate a new church. Bishop Wayman commented, "It was a fine little church."[113] William F. Williams was the pastor. From this we know that the church was organized some time before June 12, 1870. This is the earliest mention of the church found in our research.

In 1873 church trustees Abraham LeCato, Nathaniel Collins, James Finney, Jesse Stran, John Parker, Samuel Boggs, Caleb Taylor, Teagle Kellam, and Tully Phillips recorded the deed for the land purchased from George and Nancy Mason on Kitten Branch Road, across the road from the present church.[114] The only reminder

Gaskins Chapel A. M. E. Church

Old Gaskin Cemetery on Kitten Branch Road

that Gaskins Chapel ever stood at its original location is the cemetery on Kitten Branch Road.

In the early 1900s, Gaskins Chapel officials purchased land on Savageville Road and in 1902 moved the church. In 1905 the towers were built on Gaskin's Chapel, which was part of the Savageville Circuit.[115]

The cornerstone for an extension at Gaskins Chapel A. M. E. Church was laid on April 23, 1962. The Mystic Masonic Lodge No. 4 AF & A M Scottish Rite of Onancock was in charge of the service.

GRACE INDEPENDENT METHODIST CHURCH, WACHAPREAGUE

Grace Independent Methodist Church was founded in 1883 by a few members who had left Burton Chapel Methodist Church to form another church. The break had not come because of a disagreement, but because these members lived in Wachapreague, at a distance from Burton. A white church in Wachapreague moved to a new location in Bradford Neck and gave a lot and an old school building to the new organization. Through the ingenuity of church member John Elliott, a carpenter, the old building was turned into a church. Early members were Isaac Davis, Mrs. Charles Davis; John Davis; Richard B. Stephens; Edward Custis; George T. LeCato; John Bailey Sr.; John Bailey; Louisa LeCato; Susan Davis; Mary Burton; Georgiana Burton; Cora Beach; Arinthia Beach; Sarah Beach; and John Elliott.

The new church was named Powelltown Methodist Mission. The church used this name until 1910 when the name was changed to Grace Methodist Church. The congregation worshipped in the original building until 1910 when a new structure was erected. Over the years, a new pastor's study, church offices, and choir rooms were added.[116]

Grace Independent Methodist Church

JERUSALEM BAPTIST CHURCH, TEMPERANCEVILLE

Jerusalem Baptist Church was founded by Reverend James Cluff (see photo page 43) of Chincoteague, a former slave and soldier in Company A, 1st Eastern Virginia Infantry during the Civil War. When slavery was over, Reverend Cluff moved from the island of Chincoteague to what is now Temperanceville and began spreading the word of God. The congregation of Jerusalem worshipped under a tent until a storm destroyed this makeshift church, and Jerusalem was forced to build a church. It is said that Rev Cluff sold eggs, butter, and farm produce door-to-door to earn enough money to build Jerusalem.

In 1878 Cluff, along with Issac Justice, Levin Handy, John Copes, Hank Copes, Spencer Copes, and Jena Justice, church trustees, purchased two acres of land from Albert S. and Anna S. Matthews. The deed included an agreement that the congregation could be built a church on the property and Sunday School could be held at the church, but a condition of the sale was

Jerusalem Baptist Church

that the church could not build a school for black children on the land. Although Jerusalem Baptist Church agreed to the condition at the time, the community needed a school for black children.[117] In 1895 Jerusalem entered into a deed of exchange with Accomack County for land on which to build the Jerusalem Elementary School. In 1964 Jerusalem bought back the Jerusalem Elementary School from the Accomack County School Board. A portion of the school building suffered from serious disrepair, and Jerusalem moved the usable part to the church, where it was attached and veneered with the church to give the appearance of one building.[118]

When Cluff resigned from Jerusalem and was replaced by Reverend Perham, he went to other towns and hamlets preaching. He led Tabernacle Baptist Church in Horntown, Christ Union Baptist Church in Chincoteague, Mount Sinai Baptist Church in New Church, and Mount Olive Baptist Church in Jenkins Bridge. Late in his life he returned to Jerusalem and spent his final years in the church that lived because of him. The closeness of the churches organized by Cluff may be seen years after his death when Christ Union Baptist Church on Chincoteague disbanded and several of the members made Jerusalem their new church home.[119]

MACEDONIA A. M. E. CHURCH, ACCOMAC

Reverend James H. A. Johnson of the Baltimore Annual Conference was the first missionary in this area, beginning in 1865, soon after the close of the Civil War. On Wednesday morning, December 20, 1865, he landed at Cherrystone, Northampton County, Virginia. A week later, on December 27, he led a meeting to organize the first African Methodist Episcopal Church on the Eastern Shore of Virginia at Drummond-town. Eighteen members were present at that meeting, among them Henry and Rachel Wharton and George Custis. The sermon on this occasion was from the 62nd Psalm, 8th verse.[120]

Most black churches of this era were organized and gathered under oak trees or bush bowers, but Macedonia A. M. E. took up residence in the Drummond Town

Macedonia A. M. E. Church

Methodist Episcopal Church, a white church that had been confiscated by the Union troops early in the Civil War. Macedonia worshiped in this church until the Freedmen's Bureau allowed land to be returned to pre-war owners.

Macedonia A. M. E. Church purchased land to build a church from Isaac Satchell; the church was built in 1889.[121] Under the guidance of Reverend A. R. Montague, Macedonia A. M. E. Church was renovated in 1909. In 1974, under the leadership of Reverend William H. Grant Jr., it was rebuilt. The present church, built in 1988 during the tenure of Reverend S. L. Hayward, connects to the old church, which is still usable.[122]

METOMPKIN BAPTIST CHURCH, PARKSLEY

The Metompkin Baptist Church was founded in 1877 by Reverend Abel J. Satchell

Metompkin Baptist Church

and a few interested members. The church was built of logs and hewn logs in a maze of bushes and undergrowth off what is now U. S. Route 13, about a mile east of the present building.

Satchell served Metompkin until his death. Before his death, he designated

Reverend Thomas Turlington, a local minister, to lead the church.[123]

Between 1914 and 1915, the original building underwent a complete renovation program and took on a completely new look.

In 1924 Reverend J. C. Bond of Elizabeth City, North Carolina, started a building program. By 1947, at the time of Bond's death, a baptismal pool had been added, a basement dug, rooms added to the rear of the church, and a parsonage purchased.

In 1948 Reverend J. M. Douglas began a seventeen year tenure. During Douglas's administration, Metompkin underwent an extensive building program. The auditorium was modernized, an educational building completed and equipped, and the grounds landscaped.[124, 125]

METROPOLITAN UNITED METHODIST CHURCH, BAYSIDE

Founded under the administration of Reverend Isaiah Johnson, Metropolitan United Methodist Church, first called Johnson Metropolitan Methodist Church, was organized in 1870. The present structure, built in 1899, was preceded by the original church, which was built shortly after its founding. During this time, the parsonage was also purchased. The church trustees who worked on these projects were Benjamin T. Coard, William Douglas Young, Noah Wise, John H. Hall, Henry White, Purnell Drummond, William Savage, Alfred Chandler, and Oswald Finney.[126]

In 1897 Metropolitan and Adams Methodist churches joined to buy land for a parsonage to serve both churches.[127]

Metropolitan United Methodist Church

MOUNT NEBO BAPTIST CHURCH, SLUTKILL NECK

Reverend Thomas Turlington, a former slave and founder of several Baptist churches, organized Mount Nebo Baptist Church in 1881. Mount Nebo trustees Ezekiel Johnson, Edward Chandler, and Letie Turner purchased an acre of land from John Savage in Slutkill Neck in 1891. It is not know when the church was built.Mount Nebo is one of a very few churches on the Eastern Shore that continues to meet in the orginal structure.[128]

Thomas Turlington

Mt. Nebo has always been a small church because it is located in a sparcely populated area. Althouth it was small it organized quickly with John Turner and Viola Paddy as Sunday School teachers. Viola Paddy was also the first church clerk.

The church is on property ajacent to the elementary school of the same name. Many of the church members attended the school and, when the school was closed and the children sent to Savageville, the church used the school as a hall.[129]

Mount Nebo Baptist Church in 2006

An Early Mount Nebo Baptist Church

Mount Olive Baptist Church, Hacks Neck

Mount Olive Baptist Church in Hacks Neck was organized as a Methodist Church by several members of the Sample family, including Frank R. and Obediah Sample in 1897. At the end of that year trustees Alexander Ames, James Sample, and Isaac Sample purchased an acre of land from Francis T. and Ann E. Boggs in Hacks Neck to build the Mount Olive Methodist Church.[130]

In 1926, the members of the Church decided that they no longer wished to remain in the Methodist Conference, and the Church changed its religious affiliation to Baptist and became known as the Second Mount Olive Baptist Church.

Reverend Fred Gunter was called as pastor in 1926 and served until 1956. In 1960 Gunter was succeeded by his son Reverend Joseph Gunter, who served until 1963. In 1964, Reverend G. W. Revell was called as pastor. The church cornerstone attests to the beginning of two churches, a Methodist one in 1897 and a Baptist one in 1927.[131]

Recently rededicated as New Mount Olive Baptist

When the congregation dwindled, the church closed. Later it opened for a time as Pungoteague Community Church under the direction of Bishop J. W. Kellam. Most recently the church has been opened by the descendants of the founding Sample family, and rededicated as New Mount Zion Baptist Church.

The building adjacent to the church is used as a hall. Although it is thought be the old Hacks Neck School, it is a dwelling donated to the church and moved there within the last thirty years. The Hacks Neck School was located across the road from the church and burned many years ago.[132]

MOUNT OLIVE BAPTIST CHURCH, JENKINS BRIDGE

In 1887, John S. Gaskins and his son, Meshach Gaskins, sold a half acre of land to Obed Godwin and James H. Holden, the trustees of Mount Olive Baptist Church, and Reverend James Cluff. In the deed, Mount Olive was called Mount Holly Baptist Church, possibly an error in the recording.[133]

Although of different religious denominations, Mount Olive Baptist and Saint John's Methodist Episcopal Church have shared not only a neck of land, but devotion to their community. It was Mount Olive Baptist Church that leased the land to Accomack School Board on which the Saint John's Elementary School was built. In 1907 trustees of both churches Dennis Fletcher, James Johnson, George Mason, John Mason, Lewis Hargis, James Holden, Nathaniel Holden, Obed Godwin, and Peace Milburn purchased land from Sallie R. Marshall and Thomas E. Marshall near Pocomoke Methodist Church, South, to be used as a cemetery.[134]

Mount Zion A. M. E. Church, Jamesville

Mount Zion A. M. E. Church was founded in 1870 in Jamesville by Reverend John Henry Offer during his first assignment to the Eastern Shore. In July, 1870, the church trustees Smith Giddings and Jasper Heath purchased from Herman Haupt and his wife Ann Cecelia of Philadelphia land located on Occahonnock Neck Road and Battle Point Road on which to build a church.

The agreement to purchase the land differed from most deeds in that the Haupts reserved the rights to the timber and included a clause stating:

the express reservation and condition that if said congregation of Zions Church shall not conduct their worship in an orderly and proper manner, or if the neighbourhood shall be disturbed or tresspass is committed upon adjacent properties, then and in that event the said Ann Cecelia Haupt reserves the right to revoke and cancel this deed and within three months and shall remove their building from the property

In 1889 the Mt. Zion Church was rebuilt under the pastorate of Reverend I. L. Butt. Repairs were made fifteen years later, when Reverend William R. White made them one of his priorities.

In 1905 Mount Zion A. M. E. and St Joseph A. M. E. joined together in purchasing a lot to build a parsonage at Belle Haven. It is not known how long the church survived.[135]

Mount Zion Plat

Mount Zion A. M. E. Church, Treherneville

On the Bridgetown Circuit, Mount Zion A. M. E. in Treherneville was organized in 1870, but the church wasn't erected until 1905. In 1961 Mount Zion was remodeled

The congregation of Mount Zion A. M. E. Church in Treherneville was always small but had so dwindled until in 2002 the church could no longer sustain itself. The remaining membership was absorbed into Shorters Chapel A. M. E. Church. The former Mount Zion A. M. E. Church building is now used by the New Mission United Methodist Church. The cemetery in Treherneville that once served Mount Zion A. M. E. now serves members of Shorters Chapel, the former members of Mount Zion.[136]

Mount Zion A. M. E. Church, Treherneville

New Allen Memorial A. M. E. Church, Franktown

The Pine Tree Mission at Franktown was established on April 20, 1869. This was the forerunner of New Allen Memorial African Methodist Episcopal Church of Franktown. Pine Tree Mission was the tangible result of the combined determination, sacrifice, cooperation, and hard work of a few pioneering individuals. The first construction was a bower, with poles along the sides to support a thatched roof of shrubbery. Members prepared for the construction of a more stable building by gathering logs, making pegs, constructing furniture, and planning to complete and occupy their first church building. At first, the membership was served by pastors from neighboring churches.[137]

Pine Tree Mission grew, and it was from this church that the Allen Chapel was born, named for Richard Allen, founder of the first A. M. E. Church.

In 1870 George E. Francis, Alfred Wallace, Alfred Hudson, Joseph Church, England Mills, John Turner, and George Church, early trustees of Allen Chapel, purchased one acre of land from James Savage.

Early Allen Chapel A. M. E.

New Allen Memorial A. M. E. Church

During its first decade the church grew under the leadership of such ministers as Reverend Thomas Cole, spiritual leader of the Pungoteague Circuit; Reverend R. Govans, under whom Franktown was elevated to "station" status by the Conference; Reverend J. H. Offer, who proved to be an effective leader and great organizer; and Reverend S. M. Copeland.[138]

The congregation outgrew the boundaries of their first church just at the time that the Wardtown Baptist Church, a white church, disbanded. It had been said that Allen Chapel purchased the Baptist church and moved it to Franktown, but neither the church history and nor interviews reflect such a purchase.

Over the years the church was raised, refurbished, bricked over, and renamed the New Allen Memorial A. M. E. Church.

New Mount Calvary Baptist Church, Bacon Hill

During 1896, Deacons George Lecator and George Shields met with George Annis and his wife Emma to organize the Mount Calvary Baptist Church at Bacon Hill.

After land was purchased, plans were made to erect a church. The church was built by Reverends Isaac Lee and Levi Duncan, and Deacon Henry Toliver. Reverend Charles J. Henry of Snow Hill, Maryland, was called to pastor the Mount Calvary Baptist Church. On the fourth Sunday of September, 1897, the first service was held, and Mount Calvary Baptist Church began to serve the community.

The original church construction was very rudimentary: the walls were made of rails of wood, the seats were made of hewed trees, and the pulpit was a length of wood. Despite the rough physical edifice, the church supplied this congregation and community with spiritual direction for 31 years.

In 1928, under the leadership of Reverend A. D. Weaver of Portsmouth, Virginia, Mount Calvary Baptist Church was rebuilt to increase the floor space and to add triple-pane stained glass windows, plaster walls, a new pulpit, and a new steeple with a brass bell. This new church was then referred to as New Mount Calvary

Baptist Church. During this period, Weaver also led New Mount Zion in Painter. He held church services in the morning at New Mount Zion Baptist and in the afternoon at New Mount Calvary.

In 1945, Reverend D.E. Hardy was called to lead the church. Under his direction, light fixtures were added, the ceiling lowered, and a heating system with central air installed.

Mount Calvary Baptist Church

Under the administration of present pastor Reverend Smith, in June 2002, the church underwent a complete facelift. To the annex were added three classrooms, a finance room, a choir room, and a recording studio.[139]

NEW MT. ZION BAPTIST CHURCH, PAINTER

The New Mount Zion Baptist Church was organized on the first Sunday in September, 1881, when about thirty individuals withdrew from Shiloh Baptist Church and formed Mount Zion Baptist. At that time, there was no building for church services, so the members built a bush bower.

The first deacons were James H. Smith, Harry Savage, Samuel Scarbrough, Henry Fosque, Abraham Jones, Levin Ayres, and George Rogers. Some of the members at that first worship service were: Peter Tankard, Henry Francis, Lettie Rogers, Irene LeCato, May Smith, Ellen Bell, Isabelle Jubilee, Donna Smith, Emma Heath, Henny Ayers, Henny Harmon, Tennie Burton, Jane Jubilee, Ann Mapp, Ann Fletcher, Louisa Smith, Rachell Fosque, and Carlania Savage.

The church having organized, the congregation took the next step by erecting a ten-foot-square building on land purchased on Coal Kiln Road. Church trustees were George LeCato, James Smith, Henry Foskey, Delaware Kellam, Harry Savage, George Rogers, Thomas Watson, and G. W. Bradford. At that time, the church did not have a regular pastor, and various ministers were called to supply the pulpit.

Reverend Jasper Savage, former slave and founder of the Ebenezer Baptist Church in Wardtown, was in charge of the first baptizing, which took place at Round Rock, a creek east of the church, with five baptismal candidates.

Reverend Levi Duncan, also a former slave, was the first regular pastor of the church. Under his leadership another ten-foot section was added to the old structure, doubling its area. As the membership continued to grow, congregation decided to build a larger church and convert the old church into a school. Reverend Isaiah Arnold assumed leadership in 1910, and in 1913 the church was remodeled.

Reverend Patterson followed Arnold. During his time the New Mount Zion Accomack County Public School was built.

New Mount Zion Baptist Church

In 1922, Reverend A. D. Weaver was called to assume pastorial duties. During his term, two rooms were added to the church, new furniture was bought for the pulpit, a half acre of land was purchased for a cemetery, and a baptising pool was installed.

A 1944 storm destroyed the church, which was then forced to hold services in the Fisherman's Lodge Hall. The members began to work toward the construction of a new building, which was started under leadership of Reverend A. D. Weaver. This building was enclosed by the time Weaver's health began to fail. Weaver served faithfully for approximately twenty years.

The church was completed during Reverend Dennis Haughton's seventeen years of service. A heating system was installed, and pews added.

New Mount Zion Baptist Church

Reverend James Burrell became pastor in 1964. Under Burrell's guidance, the New Mount Zion Accomack County Public School building was purchased from the Accomack County School Board. The school building was used as the church hall, kitchen, and dining room. In 1992 during the administration of Reverend Willie Carter, all remnants of church and community history were discarded in favor of a modern brick church. [140, 141]

Saint Joseph A. M. E. Church, Belle Haven

Undoutedly Saint Joseph A. M. E. Church was organized under the watchful eye of Reverend John Henry Offer during his first assignment to the Eastern Shore.

Little is known about the Saint Joseph A. M. E. Church site at Belle Haven except A. M. E. Records mention that Reverend William Jerome White spent two years here and laid the corner-stone for a new church in 1897. However the cornerstone does not mention White, but rather shows the term of A. Ward, 8th Pastor, 1897-1947.

A sign on the front of Saint Joseph A. M. E. tells that the church has service on the 2nd and 4th Sundays of each month.[142]

Saint Joseph A. M. E. Church, Belle

Saint Paul A. M. E. Church, Pungoteague

Oral history says this church began across the street from where it is now located. Perusal of the cemetery bears witness to its use as early as 1868, for here is buried Reverend Charles Case, who church members say was the first minister of this church. Case was born free and records show he lived his entire life in the Pungoteague area.

In 1883, Saint Paul A. M. E. trustees Severn Bevans Sr., Willam Sample, and

Levi Nock purchased a lot from William and Sarah Downing, a second piece of land which extended their property and increased the size of cemetery. The church trustees also purchased two-thirds ownership of the Fisherman Lodge and Lone Star Lodge Hall on the adjacent property, when Fisherman's disbanded. St Paul's A. M. E. Church to the south, the Lone Star Masonic Lodge in the middle, and the Pungoteague Elementary School to the north on adjoining properties constituted a local African American community.[143]

Saint Paul's A. M. E. Church

SHILOH BAPTIST CHURCH, BOSTON

Shiloh Baptist Church in Boston, founded in 1878 under the leadership of Reverend T. W. Nettles, is considered the mother church for several south Accomack Baptist churches. In 1881 Shiloh released several members to form the Mount Zion Baptist Church in Painter. Shiloh Baptist is also the mother church of the Holy Trinity Baptist Church in Pungoteague. Although founded five years before Shiloh, Ebenezer Baptist Church was also assisted by Shiloh members transferring to bolster the

Ebenezer membership. Many years ago, members of Shiloh moved to or near Wardtown and joined the Ebenezer Baptist Church, which was at that time a small church.

Over the years the original church structure was replaced twice due to fire. It was rebuilt in 1904 and 1907. The present structure is almost 100 years old and during that time changes and additions have been made to the building.[144]

Shiloh Baptist Church

ST. JOHN BAPTIST CHURCH, ONANCOCK

In 1887 Samuel Wise, William Matthews, and Samuel Nock purchased from Edward L. East an acre of land for $42.00 in Onancock. The land is located on the south side of Church Street, separated from Pine Street by a Masonic Hall lot. Two months after the purchase, on October 8, 1887, St. John Baptist Church trustees applied to the American Baptist Home Mission for a loan of $250.00 to build a church.[145]

St. John Baptist Church

ST. JOHN'S METHODIST CHURCH, MESSONGO

St. John's Methodist Church was founded in 1876 under direction of the Delaware Methodist Conference. In September 1876 William T. Bloxom and his wife, Nancy M. Bloxom, sold to Levi Northam, Samuel Logan, Dennis Fletcher, James Johnson, George Duncan, Benjamin Fletcher, and James Bowen, trustees of the newly formed church, about 3/8 acre of land in Pocomoke Neck on a road then called "Long Road," now Withams Road.[146] This church was built in 1876 and rebuilt in 1941.

St. John's Methodist

St. John's Methodist and nearby Mount Olive Baptist Church acted in concert in many areas. Mount Olive Baptist Church leased land to the Accomack School Board on which St. John's Elementary School was built. In 1907 trustees of both churches Dennis Fletcher, James Johnson, George Mason, John Mason, Lewis Hargis, James Holden, Nathaniel Holden, Obed Godwin, and Peace Milburn purchased land from Sallie R. Marshall and Thomas E. Marshall near Pocomoke Methodist Church South to be used as a cemetery. [147]

St. Luke A. M. E. Church, Daugherty

On May 26, 1872, St. Luke A. M. E. Church trustees Thomas Garrison, Benjamin Parramore, William Baylie, Samuel Nock, and Robert Hackett purchased 1/2 acre of land from John Coleburn of Locust Mount. Exactly when the church was built is unknown, but an old church history estimates 1872, the year of the land acquisition. Later the church purchased land on which parsonage was built.

Accomack County Court records show that in 1904 St. Luke A. M. E. Church notified the court of new trustees: Levi Conquest, Jacob Stratton, John Hagly, James H. Allen, Abel Satchell, Nathaniel Bagwell, Edgar Taylor, Alexander Taylor, and Charlie Riddick.

St. Luke A. M. E. Church

In 1956, St. Luke Trustees Henry Harmon, Thomas Ewell, Elias Young, Francis Taylor, Stanford Allen, and John D. Allen purchased the Daugherty Elementary School building to use as a hall. The church has always promoted healthful recreation for the youth of the church. In keeping with the motto "Save the boys today, you will not have to worry about the men of tomorrow," St. Luke sponsored Boy Scout Troop No. 862.[148, 149]

Lodge Hall, Daugherty Elementary School, and St. Luke Church Hall

65

St. Stephen's A.M.E. Church, Cape Charles

Located on Jefferson Avenue in Cape Charles, St. Stephen's is the only A. M. E. Church in the town and the only African Methodist Episcopal Church organized without the aid of Reverend John H. Offer. The church congregation met in a building vacated when Bethany Methodist Church moved into a new building. In 1894

St. Stephens A.M.E. Church

Cape Charles School District 4 purchased the building and Lot 378 and used it as a school. In the same year the school division resold the lot to the William L. Scott Estate. Meanwhile, St. Stephens continued to use the building as a church.

Although this church was organized in 1888, it was not until 1912 that Mathew H. Taylor, Charles H. Strong, and Edward Mehl, the surviving trustees of the Scott estate, sold to John Knock, Thomas Floyd, Charles Stephens, William Turpin, and Thomas Skinner, trustees of Saint Stephen's A. M. E. Church. The church building once used as a school was moved to Lot 51 on Jefferson Avenue. [150]

Over the years, St. Stephen's purchased two additional lots to expand the church's offerings to the community. [151, 152]

Shorter's Chapel A.M.E. Church, Bridgetown

Bishop James A. Shorter

Shorter's Chapel was one of the churches organized by Reverend John H. Offer circa 1870 during his tenure as the first black Methodist minister on the Eastern Shore of Virginia. It was named for the African Methodist Episcopal Bishop James A. Shorter.

Shorter's Chapel building was originally occupied by Bridgetown School. A cornerstone records the year 1883 as the year the church was constructed, but it seems likely that the Shorter's Chapel congregation predates the cornerstone and that the cornerstone actually records the building of the first addition to the church. Over the years, the church added onto the original building, increasing the size of the church over the original foundation. In 1896 the Bridgetown School trustees executed a deed of gift and gave Shorter's Chapel the school and a lot 20 x 30 feet.

Shorter's Chapel A. M. E. Church

Although a deed of gift from the trustees of the Bridgetown Elementary School transferred the ownership of the Shorter's Chapel property in 1896, the cornerstone of the church dated 1883 together with the oral history of the church confirms that the transfer of property was but a legal formality. The Bridgetown School had moved before 1883, and Shorter's Chapel occupied this space thirteen years before deed was executed.[153]

SNEAD'S MEMORIAL UNITED METHODIST CHURCH, AMES RIDGE

Snead's Memorial Methodist Church was founded in 1881 by Reverend R. J. Waters of the Delaware/Pennsylvania Methodist Conference. Reverend Waters also served as the first pastor. The half acre of land for the church was purchased in 1882 by Edmund Coleburn, Richard Davis, Abram Hateny, John Kellam, and Isaac Turlington, trustees from Margaret E. Smith, her daughters Margaret and Susan, and Susan's husband J. Fosque. The land was described as being on Ames Ridge County Road.[154]

Like several other churches Snead's fell into rather desperate financial condition in the late 1920s and 1930s, and the church property was sold at public auction. On June 9, 1936, Elmer W. Somers conveyed the ownership of Snead's Methodist Church to the Eastern Shore Citizens Bank. In 1940 the Eastern Shore Citizens Bank sold it for $750.00 to the Board of Home

Snead's United Methodist Church

Missions and Church Extension of the Methodist Episcopal Church with the general warranty of the title of Snead's Church. Not until October 1945 were the Snead Methodist Episcopal Church trustees Milton Mathews, Addie Addison, Anna Belle Ward, Abel Palmer, Arthur Read, Thomas Harmon, John Wise, George T. Hateney, and Arthur Taylor able to reclaim ownership of the church. [155]

Snead's Memorial United Methodist church is now building an addition.

SPENCE CHAPEL METHODIST CHURCH, EXMORE

When, at the end of the 1800s, the growing black population of Exmore had no place for worship, Comfort Brickhouse opened her home as a place to gather for weekly prayer and Bible study.

In 1895 Reverend John Waters of the Delaware Conference worked with this group to find a permanent place of worship. Under Waters' leadership, a plot of land was purchased from William H. Brickhouse of Hare Valley. During that year a small house of worship was constructed, which became known as the John Wesley M. E. Church. Henry Baines, Amanda Young, Martha Twyford, Essie Harmon, Peter Johns, and T. Savage were among the founders.

In October 1923, the church was completely destroyed by fire. Unfortunately, the Church had no fire insurance coverage, and the church could not be rebuilt. The congregation was forced to acknowledge that very few members had any interest in assuming the obligation of replacing the building. As time went on, members of the John Wesley M. E. Church drifted to other churches and other denominations. They abandoned the church and also their dead who were buried in the cemetery near the church. In 1949, Cox Distributing Company purchased the church property and discovered the cemetery. Holland's Funeral Home exhumed the bodies and buried them in the Union Baptist Church cemetery in Eastville.

In 1947 Reverend Oliver Spence, the District Superintendent of the Salisbury District, led a crusade for churches in need of places to worship and decided that there was a need to re-establish the Exmore church. The first church lot had been sold; a replacement lot was donated by C. J. Prettyman Sr., on Sixth Street in Lincoln Manor Community, a subdivision in Exmore.

In August of 1947, former members of the John Wesley M. E. Church began meeting at the home of Charles Reid. After some time, Reverend William Milburn was assigned as minister and a house was rented to serve as a temporary church. Later, the Home Mission Board of the Methodist Church granted a loan to the church for a lot, and a new church building was constructed on the property. Service was held in the new building in October, 1948. [156]

Unfortunately the church was unable to sustain itself and later closed.

TABERNACLE BAPTIST CHURCH, HORNTOWN

On June 23, 1892, William T. Parks Jr., and his wife E. Addie Parks sold a half acre of land to Louis H. P. Douglas, Henry Cropper, and Preeson Roberts, trustees of the newly organized Douglas Tabernacle Baptist Church in Horntown, for $25.00. Although the deed was made in 1892 and the land was transferred in that year, the deed was not recorded in Accomack County Clerk's Office until April 13, 1908.

Built in 1892, the church was adjacent to the "Free School" land. [157]

Tabernacle Baptist Church

UNION BAPTIST CHURCH, EASTVILLE

Caleb James Burris, a former slave, was the founder and first pastor of Union Baptist Church in Eastville, Virginia, the first black church on the Eastern Shore. Reverend Burris was probably the first African-American ordained minister to serve on the Eastern Shore of Virgina, having received training in Philadelphia. He was born circa 1812 a slave of the Parker/Purnell/Costin families.

Early in his life he wanted to become a minister, feeling that he had been called to serve God by preaching freedom. He was able to travel to Philadelphia by offering his owner two free friends who take his place. Here he was ordained, became pastor of the First African Church and founded the Cherry Street Baptist Church.

When exactly Burris returned to the Eastern Shore is unclear. We do know that he returned to the Eastern Shore

Rev. Caleb Burris

to build a church. He must have returned some time during the Civil War, because the Union Baptist Church was organized before the end of the war.

Meetings to organize Union Baptist Church were held in the home of Wesley and Mary Ann Stephens at Town Field. At this meeting, plans were made for securing the building materials for Union Baptist Church. Founded in 1865, this was the first black church organized on the Eastern Shore of Virginia.

In September of 1866, Samuel Bibbins and Caleb Burris purchased 23 3/4 acres in Eastville from Robert and Catharine Costin. The land is described as lying south and east of the bayside road. One half of this property became the home of Caleb Burris and his family; it became Burristown. The other half became farmland for Samuel Bibbins, who gave several acres of this land to Union Baptist Church. The first school for black children on the Eastern Shore of Virginia was held at the Burris home taught by Eugenia Davis Burris, the wife of Caleb Burris. After 1870, Eugenia Davis Burris taught black children in the church.

Union Baptist Church before 1947

The growth of Union Baptist Church spawned the organization of other black Baptist churches in Northampton County. African Baptist Church in Cheriton, for example, grew out of Union. In the beginning years, these congregations met on alternate Sundays and shared a pastor; as time went on, each church employed its own pastor. The First Baptist of Capeville was organized before the death of Burris, but he died before sanctuary was constructed.

Union Baptist Church today

Reverend Caleb Burris served Union Baptist Church from July 2, 1865, until his death in 1874 at the age of 58. Some time after Burrow's death, the Church called Reverend W. H. Corbin, a man from Accomack County as pastor.

Not long after Corbin's arrival, the members decided to build a better and larger church. Under the direction of Corbin, this second church was erected. Just as Caleb Burris had done before him, Corbin also pastored the African Baptist Church in Cheriton. He served both Union and African Baptist churches until his death in 1885.

After Corbin's death, the church called Reverend Isaac Lee, a man born in Maryland and a blacksmith by trade. During Lee's administration, the Church decided to hold service every Sunday. This decision caused Lee to devote all his time to Union Baptist Church, resigning his position as pastor of African Baptist Church.

Under Lee's leadership, the third church was built. During this period, the first organ was purchased and the first choir organized. Lee also organized the Woman's Educational and Missionary Society and the Baptist Young People's Union. Lee also served as Chairman of the first board of trustees of Tidewater Institute.

By 1900 Lee's health had begun to fail. Church members opened their homes to him as hospice. He died in 1910.

After the death of Lee, the church called Reverend F. B. Mitchell. During Mitchell's pastorate, the church was closed three times due to influenza epidemics. Several churches suffered this fate. This caused the church to suffer some financial reversals. After several years of influenza openings and closings, Mitchell resigned.

In 1917 Reverend C. H. Morton was called to pastor Union Baptist Church. Morton had been the principal of Corey Institute. During Morton's administration, two rooms were added to the church, one for the pastor's study and one for the choir. The old church parsonage and four acres of land on which the parsonage was located were bought and paid for.

Morton served as pastor for twenty-two years, until his health began to fail. In January of 1939, he resigned as pastor of Union Baptist Church. In May, 1940, the Church called Reverend Y. B. Williams.

On Sunday morning November 30, 1947, Union Baptist Church caught fire, and the entire Church was destroyed. In August, 1948, Williams accepted a call to the First African Baptist Church in Richmond, Virginia, and left the Eastern Shore.

Fund-raisers were held, and each member made a pledge of money. The men of the church, using their own tractors and equipment, dug the basement, and, after a period of eighteen months, the congregation returned to the new structure to worship in the basement.

Reverend W. Tycer Nelson, College Minister and Associate Professor of Rural Sociology at Maryland State College, Princess Anne, Maryland, was voted by the Church to be a "supply pastor" on August 4, 1950. Nelson supplied the Union Baptist Church pulpit until his resignation in 1964. During his fourteen year, tenure as pastor of Union Baptist Church, Nelson oversaw the rebuilding of Union Baptist Church and the beginnings of a new parsonage.

Reverend H. L. Long came to pastor Union Baptist Church in 1964. During Long's six-year tenure at Union Baptist Church, the new parsonage was completed. Also renovations were completed on the sanctuary including lowering the ceiling and the installation of acoustical tiles.

In 1972 Reverend W. C. Rucker became the pastor of Union Baptist Church. During his administration, the annex was added to house new bathrooms to the front area of the church. [158, 159]

4 Lodges and Fraternal Organizations

One of the earliest needs of humankind was to form connections with one another, first for protection, later for social purposes. During the founding of this country, various elements of the citizenry created clubs and secret organizations. Before Africans were brought to this country, they aspired to membership in groups within their individual tribes. After they were imported to North America, they saw the white population's reliance on these organizations, and they remembered stories passed down by ancestors of the secret societies they had lost in Africa.

When African slaves were emancipated by the Civil War, they were suddenly faced with the challenge of supporting themselves and their families. The first systems of support to be organized within the African-American community were churches, schools, and lodges. It seems natural through example and remembrance that one of the methods of support was fraternal organizations. These institutions emerged almost simultaneously.

The first African-American church founded on the Eastern Shore was Union Baptist Church in 1865 located in Eastville, and within that church was a school. The second church, Wayman's Chapel, founded in 1867, and later renamed Bethel A. M. E., was organized at the Lincoln School, which was the first public school for black children and funded by the Freedmen's Bureau. When the Lincoln School in Eastville outgrew its walls, the Odd Fellows Lodge # 3233 provided space for the school within its hall. The same was true with the Macedonia Masons in Accomac.

Numerous fraternal groups were founded and flourished in the two Eastern Shore counties during and after the Reconstruction Period. The first was the Grand Order of the Republic, an organization whose membership was confined to Civil War Veterans and the Women's Relief Corp, an auxiliary to the G. A. R. Then came the Odd Fellows, the Tents, the Good Samaritans, the Society of the Rehoboth, and the Masons. These early groups fostered beliefs in good health, good moral conduct, brotherly/sisterly camaraderie, and obligation to their racial community. Their benevolent acts included donating money to schools and churches, providing space in their halls for schools, providing charity to sick and indigent members, paying medical bills, and providing death and burial benefits to the families of deceased members.

In the years just before and after 1900, black families sought help from these groups when their sons were wrongly accused of crimes against the white population. Such situations forced them to secure legal representation or take flight from the community. The fraternal organizations provided the most important refuge of all, the feeling of security in numbers.

Lodge Hall and Storehouse, Eastville

Old Eastville Store House has a long history of housing African-American businesses and organizations. In 1887 Smith Brickhouse and his wife, Cornelia, purchased this old store house, which stands on a quarter of an acre, from James T. Heath. Brickhouse and his wife Cornelia defaulted on the loan, and in 1888 the property went up for public auction. In 1890 it was purchased by Southey T. Collins, Harry H. Up-

Old Eastville Storehouse

shur, and William M. Fitchett, the trustees of the Grand Order of the Odd Fellows #2774. From 1890 to 1936, the building was the home of the Odd Fellows, the Pride of Virginia Masonic Lodge No. 18, Roselle's Barber Shop, and Miss Sue's Cook Shop owned by Sue Winder. The building's unusual configuration is the result of a 1936 requirement by the town of Eastville that buildings be moved so sidewalk could be laid. The Odd Fellows could not afford to move the building, and it was sold to Howard Adams to be used as his law office. To circumvent the new town ordinance of building setbacks, the top floor was braced and the first floor of the building was cut back to accommodate the new sidewalk. It is now owned by the Northampton Insurance Company.[160]

PRIDE OF VIRGINIA MASONIC LODGE #18, EASTVILLE

When the old Brickhouse storehouse was sold in 1936, the Grand Order of the Odd Fellows #2774 and Pride of Virginia Masonic Lodge #18 were left without a meeting place. In 1937 the Odd Fellows purchased property from H. P. and Lula James. It is not known when they constructed their lodge hall, but in 1941 it appears that the Odd Fellows #2774 disbanded and several of their members joined the Odd Fellows #3233. Grand Order of the Odd Fellows #2774 trustees Solomon Jacobs, Joseph G. Collins, and Albert Thomas sold the property to the Pride of Virginia #18 trustees James C. Allen, Charles N. McCune, and William Medley.[161]

Pride of Virginia #18

Mystic Masonic Lodge, Savageville

Mystic Masonic Lodge

In 1902 the Mystic Masonic Lodge trustees Smith Ames, George Ames, Charles C. Becket, Henry A. Wise, and William A. Gunter purchased land from Riley and Nelly B. Joynes and Samuel L. Burton for the purpose of building a lodge hall in Savageville. The lodge disbanded some years ago.[162]

Odd Fellows Lodge Hall, Eastville

The Odd Fellows Lodge #3233 was founded in the 1890s. Their lodge hall was built in 1911. This lodge was one of two Odd Fellows organizations in Eastville. The building served as more than a meeting place for the Odd Fellows~it accommodated the overflow of African-American children from the Eastville School as well. By the 1950s many of the members had died off. The vacant building became the business and home of Clem Bell's Radio and Television Repair Service. Since Bell's demise, the once busy building is now vacant.[163]

Odd Fellows Lodge #3222

Grand Army of the Republic, Eastville

Grand Army of the Republic was the oldest black fraternal organization in Northampton County. It was made up of veterans of the Union Army. In 1886 Robert J. Satchell, Arthur Booker, George Cottrell, and Alfred Riley, acting on the behalf of the GAR Post #18 and the Good Samaritans #85, purchased one acre from Robert and Catherine Costin for purposes of constructing their meeting place. The land was a portion of the Kendall Grove farm and was near the gate leading from the farm to Eastville. This building was demolished in 2004.[164]

Grand Army of the Republic

Macedonia Masonic Lodge #19, Accomac

Drummondtown Lodge of Odd Fellows trustees Littleton D. Wharton, Theodore Wise, William Drummond, John Gray, George W. Perkins, and Benjamin Coard purchased a quarter acre from Isaac Satchell in 1882 in Drummondtown on what is

Old Macedonia Masonic Hall #19

Macedonia Masonic Lodge #19

77

now Church Road. This organization became a part of a growing and developing community. They provided space for a school and created a place where their members could be buried by creating the Odd Fellows Cemetery. During the 1940s the number of Odd Fellows diminished to the point where it became necessary to disband, as eventually all Odd Fellows Lodges did. The Macedonia Masonic Lodge #19 was formed and is active today. [165]

MOUNT ZION ROYAL LODGE #8, TREHERNEVILLE

In 1913 Samuel L. Bell, John Moore, James Morris, Julius Scarborough and George Thomas, trustees of the Mount Zion Royal Masonic Lodge #8, purchased a lot of unspecified size on Treherne Road in Treherneville. The deed for this property refers to the lodge as #148, but since there are no other Masonic buildings in Treherneville it seems a clerical error which may account for misnumbering the organization. The building is in very poor repair and may be inactive.[166]

Mount Zion Royal Lodge #8

LONE STAR MASONIC LODGE #38, PUNGOTEAGUE

Lone Star Masonic Lodge

The Lone Star Masonic Lodge trustees Isaac Phillips, Caleb Taylor, and Southey Wright purchased an eighth of an acre from William Downing and Sarah his wife. The land was located in the village of Pungoteague bordered on the south by the "stage road." The land cost $12.00.

The Masonic Lodge later sold a portion of the land and the building to the Mount Olive Galilean Fisherman Lodge No. 187. When this group became inactive, the Lone Star Masonic Lodge sold two thirds interest to Saint Paul's A. M. E. Church.[167]

5 Schools

The freedmen were eager to build churches and then schools, but the Freedmen's Bureau convinced them of the wisdom of focusing on schools. However, when they attempted to purchase land, they discovered that it was owned by white citizens who were not disposed to selling land so former slaves could be educated. From the beginning of Eastern Shore involvement in the Civil War to the start of development of black education there, Samuel Chapman Armstrong was present. In 1863 he was given command of the 9th U.S. Colored Troops, a company largely comprised of Eastern Shore soldiers. In 1865 he mustered out as Brevet Brigadier-General of Volunteers, and by 1866 he was appointed Bureau Agent for the Freedmen's Bureau at Fort Monroe in Hampton, Virginia. As Freedmen's

Samuel C. Armstrong

Bureau Agent, he interacted with many Eastern Shore black people. On May 25, 1867, the local representative of the Freedmen Bureau reported to Samuel Chapman Armstrong that three day schools were in the area: one school two miles south of Eastville in Northampton County with eighteen students taught by Jennie Jacob, a local black woman; another in New Boston, four miles south of Pungoteague in Accomack County, taught by James Martin, a local black man with 20 scholars; and a third school one and a half miles north of Horntown taught by Louisa Selby. This teacher, also a local resident, could teach the children only how to spell because she was unable to read. These schools were established by their communities without aid of the Freedmen's Bureau or the American Missionary Association.

In Bridgetown, a group of freedmen purchased an acre of land and collected $80.00 toward the $250.00 needed to construct a building. Little private schools sprang up all over, with some teachers having but the most rudimentary of skills trying to provide education for black children and adults.

By the end of 1868, under the direction and protection of the Freedmen's Bureau and the American Missionary Association, the Lincoln School opened in Bridgetown near Eastville, the Smith School opened in Pungoteague, the Sherwood School in Drummondtown (now Accomac), the Armstrong School in Onancock, and the New Boston School near Little Boston. Most of the new students were also new to freedom. They brought with them few academic skills, and the buildings that housed their first scholarly experiences were drafty old places, sometimes little more than shacks.

In 1870 a public school system was created in Virginia for both black and white students. Some of the schools that had been held in churches immediately after the Civil War now became public schools. Nonetheless, the idea that "to educate a Negro is to spoil a laborer" prevailed among the white leadership throughout the South. Black children were viewed as inferior and carried the stigma of slavery. Because of these and other issues, schools for black children were funded at very low levels.

In 1915 Northampton County had five accredited white high schools. There were no high schools for black children in that county until 1935 and none until 1932 for Accomack County. The average number of white pupils per teacher was 24; the average number of black pupils was 58. The white per capita cost of instruction in the elementary grades was $9.25. The per capita cost of instruction for black children was $5.40, little more than half of the amount for the white children.

The Peabody Fund, the first philanthropic effort to help educate black children, was organized shortly after the end of the Civil War. The Peabody Fund became the model for the Slater, Jeanes, Randolph, and Rosenwald Funds.

The Jeanes Fund, named for founder Anna T. Jeanes, a Philadelphia Quaker, paid for black educators to be trained as supervisors in schools all over the South. The Eastern Shore received four Jeanes Supervisors: Margaret McCune and Cora Campbell in Northampton and Mary N. Smith and Carrie Carter in Accomack.

In the 1920s and 1930s, the Rosenwald Foundation sponsored four black elementary schools on the Shore: Cape Charles, Boston, Whitesville, and Mappsville. Each school required a sizeable contribution from the black community that attests to the importance of education in African-American life.

In the 1930s, the New Deal gave rise to the Civil Works Administration (CWA, 1933-34), the Federal Emergency Relief Administration (FERA, 1933-38), and the Works Progress Administration (1935-39) to provide jobs to unemployed workers on public projects sponsored by federal, state, and local agencies. Several schools were built in both counties under these programs.

In April of each year, Accomack and Northampton counties held Industrial Exhibits. The Accomack County Industrial Exhibit began in 1920; Northampton had started 11 years earlier, in 1909. The teachers, students, and school communities looked forward to competing with other school communities. Prizes were awarded for the five best school exhibits, which included many varied categories: chair caning, basketry, wood working, sewing, original written compositions, and advanced arithmetical problems. Entries for prize consideration were unending.

Both counties held May Day exercises, complete with entertainment for the May Queen and her court by square dancing, the Virginia Reel, and May Pole wrapping. Likewise, both counties held a Field Day; Accomack County Field Day at Tasley Fairground and Northampton County Field Day at Weirwood Fairground. Children in every school dressed in blue bottoms and white tops, gathering to perform calisthenics, run relays, and perform other daring physical feats.

In 1948, the Northampton County School Board's decision to send black children to Birdsnest School and white children to Willis Wharf and Cheriton schools brought out 500 white parents and patrons to the April 12, 1948 meeting to oppose the plan. After much discussion, a committee was formed. Members of the committee made several proposals, including one by J. W. Downing that the county not take over any more white schools for colored pupils. Most of the proposals were similar and lacked consideration of schooling for black children.

A week later, members of the committee met with the school board. A. T. Leatherbury, school board chair, and A. S. DeHaven, Northampton County School Board superintendent, addressed the committee and said that (school) housing for colored pupils in Northampton was inadequate, that there were two colored children in local schools for every white child, and that the school board faced three alternatives: (1) let the schools remain as they are; (2) float a bond issue, not knowing how long it would take to get a bond issue through; or (3) use the Birds Nest School.

Luckily for black education and for white patrons, the Hare Valley School burned. Children from the burned school were sent to New Allen Memorial A. M. E. Church for classes and a school bond passed to build a new school in the Hare Valley area.

Northampton and Accomack County schools remained segregated long after the United States Supreme Court decided *Oliver L. Brown et.al. v. the Board of Education of Topeka, Kansas* in 1954. Indeed, nearly twenty years passed before the first steps were taken to implement the federal mandate in the late 1960s. Even then, the two counties moved toward integration very slowly, in different years instituting "freedom of choice," first integrating a few black students into white schools. These black students could choose to attend a white or a black school. Oral history says that three white students freely chose a black school in Northampton and none chose to attend black schools in Accomack. The knowledge that black schools had been substandard since their beginning made it impractible to use them as an integration staging area. For years after Eastern Shore schools were integrated, segregation existed within the integrated school setting.

ACCOMACK ELEMENTARY SCHOOL SITE, ACCOMACK

Shortly after the Civil War, an elementary school was established in Drummondtown by the Freedmen's Bureau and the American Missionary Association. This school was called the Sherwood School. It is not known how long this building was used or where it was located. Some evidence indicates that the Drummondtown school, which followed the Freedmen's Bureau school, was housed in the Macedonia Masonic Lodge Hall. In 1920 the school board purchased two acres from James Wharton in an area called Rural Hill. On this land, a four-room school was built. When in 1956 the Mary Nottingham Smith High School became an elementary school, the Accomac Elementary School was closed. There is no building that marks the site.[168]

THE ALLEN SCHOOL, HARE VALLEY

The early years of education for blacks were in private schools. DeWitt Allen from Tennessee and his wife, Daisy Allen from Jamaica, British West Indies, owned and operated a private school for black children in Hare Valley and surrounding areas. Daisy Allen was the niece of Dr. Charles Read, who came to the United States in 1913[169] and was one of the first black physicians in Northampton County. The Allens operated their school until the late 1940s, when the Northampton County School Board declined to sell them text books. The tuition was .05 per day, per child.[170]

BAYSIDE ELEMENTARY SCHOOL, BAYSIDE

Built in 1922 and located in Bayside, across the road from Metropolitan Methodist Church, the Bayside Elementary School served the children of the community until South Accomack Elementary School opened in the 1960s. It then served as a church hall.[171]

Bayside Elementary School

BELLE HAVEN ELEMENTARY SCHOOL, BELLE HAVEN

Belle Haven Elementary School

Located on Big Pine Road, this school stands adjacent to the St Joseph A. M. E. Church. Very little could be found on the history of this facility.[172]

BETHANY ELEMENTARY SCHOOL, CAPE CHARLES

Bethany, the first school for black children in Cape Charles, still stands on the corner of Washington Ave. and Peach St. It was started in 1888, when the Bethany Methodist

Bethany Elementary School

Episcopal Church constructed a new sanctuary on the corner of Peach and Randolph streets. Black children immediately began using the abandoned Bethany Church as a school while Saint Stephens A. M. E. Church used it as a sanctuary. In 1894 Cape Charles School Board District 4 purchased the church building and Lot 378 from Bethany trustees Conrad Grimmer, James W. Jones, George B. Tilghman, John M. Anderson,

Charles B. Jones, Charles A. McKenny and E. Washington Milligan.[173] For reasons unknown, in that same year, Cape Charles School district 4 sold the building and Lot 378 to the estate of William Scott.[174] The school continued to hold classes and the Saint Stephens A. M. E. Church continued to meet there until 1912, when St. Stephens purchased the building from the Scott estate and moved it to Lot 51 on Jefferson Ave. Thereupon, School District 4 purchased a lot on Washington and Peach where it erected a frame building.[175] This structure is now veneered with cinderblock and is occupied by the Philadelphia Church of Christ. Laura Chapman, still living in Cape Charles at age 98, remembers attending this school, when it was a frame building. She recalls being taught by Charlotte Collins Cook and Sidney Saunders.[176]

BOSTON ELEMENTARY SCHOOL, BOSTON

Boston was the first area in Accomack County to have a black school. The New Boston School was opened in 1867 by James Martin under the auspices of the Freedmen's Bureau. Later Shiloh Baptist Church watched over the school. It is not known when the building was torn down.[177]

Boston Elementary School, a Rosenwald School

The present school was constructed in the mid-1920s with the help of the Rosenwald Foundation and it may stand on the site of the first school. The new school had four classrooms to accommodate four teachers. It was built at a total cost of $9,000, of which the black community contributed $2,500, the Accomack County School Board contributed $5,400, and the Rosenwald Foundation contributed $1100.[178] The school was in service until 1964.

BRIDGETOWN ELEMENTARY SCHOOL, BRIDGETOWN

In 1867 Bridgetown School trustees James Jacob, Peter Palmer, William Stratton, Ephram Stevens, and James Harmon purchased an acre of land from James Toy. Bridgetown Elementary School was one of the first schools established by the Freedmen's Bureau after the Civil War.[179] It stood where Shorter's Chapel A. M. E. Church stands now; the church was built on the school's foundation.

In 1896 Bridgetown School trustees exchanged land with Laban Belote for land on the north side of the road. There may have been three Bridgetown Schools--two on the present site and the original one across the road. The same day as the exchange the school trustees executed a deed of gift for a piece of land 20' x 30' on the original site so that Shorter's Chapel could have a church site.[180] In 1954 the school and 1/4 acre were sold to Viola Collins at public auction.[181]

Bridgetown Elementary School

BURTON'S ELEMENTARY SCHOOL, CHANCETOWN

The Burton's Elementary School, located across the road from Burton's Chapel Church, was built in 1922. The first school principal was Daisy Lloyd.[182] The Burton school served this community until 1964 when the new North Accomack Elementary School opened and consolidated the northern elementary schools in Accomack county.[183]

Burton's Elementary School

CAPEVILLE CONSOLIDATED ELEMENTARY SCHOOL, CAPEVILLE

Capeville Consolidated Elementary School was built as a high school for white children.[184] When the white system consolidated, the school was abandoned. In April 1946, when the Cheriton Grammar School burned, the school in Capeville was the only vacant building in the system. As plans went forth to place the Cheri

Capeville Consolidated Elementary School

ton School classes in the vacant Capeville School temporarily, some in the white community expressed displeasure at black children using a building that had been intended for white children.

Between April and September, the decision was made and plans finalized to consolidate all of the schools from Eastville south to Kiptopeake. Eight small one- and two-room schools were closed and their children sent by bus to Capeville Consolidated Elementary School. This was the first use of buses for black children on the Eastern Shore.[185]

CHEAPSIDE ELEMENTARY SCHOOL, CHEAPSIDE

Having watched schools being built in nearby villages and hamlets, the citizens of Cheapside in lower Northampton County made up their minds to have a school for their children.[186] Two acres of land were purchased in 1923, and the people went to work building their own school. The ground breaking for the school was held that year on the 4th of July. The trustees raised $5,000.00.[187] The school opened in 1923 and closed in 1946. No building remains.

CHERITON GRAMMAR SCHOOL, CHERITON

In the background of this school picture is the Cheriton Grammar School. The school was built on a quarter acre of land purchased in 1897 from Thomas and Lucy Widgeon.[188] It is not known if this was the first school constructed on the site or

Cheriton Grammar School

when this school was built. This three-room school was in use until April 1946 when it burned to the ground. The fire set in motion several years of change for the black school south of Eastville.[189]

In 1947 the land was sold to Annie Spady Bibbins, who had been a teacher at the school and lived behind it.[190]

CHERITON ELEMENTARY SCHOOL, CHERRYSTONE

In 1890, Arthur Boykin moved to the Eastern Shore with his wife, Annie and children, Arthur, Jr. and Esther. Boykins, from Hampton Institute, purchased the Huntington Estate on Cherrystone Creek from William H. Kimberly for $19,000.00. This property was to serve as a home for the Boykins family and as a school, with the farmland to help support the school. There is not much known about the school except that Cheriton Elementary School lasted only a few years and that by the turn of the century Arthur Boykin had moved to Philadelphia to work as an insurance agent.[191]

Cheriton Elementary School

CRADDOCKVILLE ELEMENTARY SCHOOL, CRADDOCKVILLE

Craddockville Elementary School

The School Board of Pungoteague purchased 2.5 acres of land from Thomas J. and Mary Custis, John S and Ella F. Davis, William and Sadie Bull, and Forest Davis on which to build this school for white children.[192] Later it was used for blacks.

Even though the Craddockville Elementary School is now delapidated and ramshackled, it still appears stately as it keeps watch over the green boxes in Craddockville.

DALBY'S ELEMENTARY SCHOOL SITE, DALBY

This building is not the original Dalby's School. Capeville School District #3 purchased one acre of land from Thomas and Sarah Scott in 1914 located on Goffigon cross road between Route 13 and Route 600. It is not known when the school was built, but it closed in 1946.

The school and a quarter acre were sold to attorney Howard H. Adams in 1947. Adams then sold it to John Watson.[193] It is not known which of its owners demolished the building. However, when it was purchased by the Fisher family in the 1950s, it was a lot without a building. The present structure was built by that family.[194, 195]

Building on the Dalby Site

EASTVILLE ELEMENTARY SCHOOL, EASTVILLE

There have been black schools in Eastville since the end of the Civil War. The first school was held in the Bethel A. M. E. Church. The first building dedicated for education was built in 1872, when the state of Virginia took over the responsibility of educating all children. When classes were too large to be held in this school building, the Odd Fellows Lodge Hall was used. It is not known when the building was constructed. The land was acquired in 1876 from Jesse N. Jarvis.

Eastville Elementary School

It was in use until 1939, when a new school was built.[196]

EASTVILLE ELEMENTARY SCHOOL, EASTVILLE

The building in the background was built circa 1939 by WPA (Work Projects Administration) workers. It was in use until 1953 when a new county high school was built for black children and the old high school was used as an elementary school. The school no longer exists.[197]

Alice Smith, Vivian Wright, Jean Francis, Leslie Smith,
teachers at the new Eastville Elementary School

EXMORE ELEMENTARY SCHOOL, EXMORE

In 1917 School District #1 purchased an acre of land from Asa and Tinnie Sample, a black couple, on the Occohannock Road leading from Wardtown to Exmore. It is not know when the building was constructed or if the structure in the picture was the first school.[198] In 1951 J. A. Shelton purchased the Exmore Elementary School; years of lack of use and attention has caused it to fall into disrepair.

Exmore School

Exmore Class in 1918

FRANKTOWN ELEMENATRY SCHOOL, FRANKTOWN

Franktown Elemenatry School

Purchased from William Wallace,[199] the lot on which Franktown Elementary School once stood is on the west side of the Bayside Road, south of Franktown. The building fell into disrepair and was demolished to make room for progress. This pile of rubble is all that remains of Franktown Elementary School. [200]

HARE VALLEY ELEMENTARY SCHOOL, HARE VALLEY

Three schools have served the Hare Valley area. The first school opened under the direction of the Freedmen's Bureau in about 1868. The small red building sat on the east side of the Bayside Road north of T. B. Road. The school closed in 1910, but the building survived into the 1930s.[201]

Hare Valley Elementary School

The second school was sponsored by the People's School of Northampton County, a group of black people acting as a school board for black education in Hare Valley. In 1909 William H. and Janie Brickhouse sold one acre of land to Chester A. Harmon, William H. Mathews, William H. Brickhouse, Joseph Church, Thomas O. Gladstone, Reuben B. Upshur, and Lloyd Wilson, trustees of the People's School of Northampton County, District Number 3. This land was located in Hare Valley on what is now the northwest corner of Bayside Road and Milton Ames Drive. Chester Allen Harmon, a trustee, was one of the first teachers to work at Hare Valley School.[202] The building was destroyed by fire in 1948. The cohesiveness of the Hare Valley community can be seen in the New Allen Memorial Church members' provision of space for children needing a school.[203]

In 1949 the Northampton County School Board decided to build a new school for black children in Hare Valley and allocated $100,000.00 for it. Also in 1949, the Northampton County School Board purchased twelve adjoining acres from Arnett and Thessa Downing.[204]

Hare Valley School closed in 1993, when the new elementary school opened near Exmore.

JAMESVILLE ELEMENTARY SCHOOL, JAMESVILLE

The land for the Jamesville Elementary School was purchased by the Senior League #5 trustees John Ashby, John Milby, and Zacariah Johnson from William T. and Emma Somers in 1915. It is not known when the school was built, but it was probably in use until 1949 when the New Hare Valley School consolidated with many northern Northampton schools.[205]

Jamesville Elementary School

Jerusalem Elementary School, Temperanceville

The land for the Jerusalem Elementary School came from the Jerusalem Baptist Church through a deed of exchange with the Atlantic School Board in 1895. The Atlantic School Board sold the school and land to the Accomack County School Board in 1922. The school closed in 1964, when the children were transferred to the North Accomack Elementary School. The Jerusalem Baptist Church purchased the building in 1964 to use as a hall. Much of the building was in disrepair and not useable. The portion of the church that is bricked was the school. *see picture of Jerusalem Baptist Church, page 53.*[206]

Little Salisbury Elementary School Site, Little Salisbury

Severn Eyre and his wife sold to Eastville School District #2 the land for the Little Salisbury School on September 7, 1881. It is not known when the school was built or if more than one structure served the children of this area. The Northampton County School Board sold the quarter acre in 1947 to Roland B. Fox.[207]

Macedonia Elementary School, Bloxom

The land on which Macedonia Elementary School was built was purchased by the Macedonia School Improvement League trustees J. H. Finney, Joseph Cropper, and Elijah Byrd in 1928 at a public auction. The cost of the land was secured by Reuben Somers, a local mortician. The school continued in operation until the 1950s when the children were sent to Mappsville Elementary School.

The Macedonia Baptist Church trustees John E. Abbott, James E. Mason, and J. A. Cobb purchased the school from the Accomack County School Board to use as a church hall in June 1951. Although no longer used as a hall, Macedonia Elementary School is still a presence in the Accomack hamlet of Macedonia just east of Bloxom.[208]

Macedonia Elementary School

MACHIPONGO ELEMENTARY SCHOOL AND
NORTHAMPTON COUNTY HIGH SCHOOL, MACHIPONGO

In the fall of 1935, the Northampton County School System took over the bankrupt Tidewater Institute at Cobb Station and for the first time provided secondary education to black children. This was the first year for Northampton County High School and it continued at the Tidewater Institute campus for six years.

In the fall of 1941, Northampton County High School was moved to Machipongo to a school built for white children.[209] The school was placed under the direction of J. F. Banks, who served as principal from 1937 to 1948. William H. Smith became principal of the high school in the fall of 1948 and served until 1967. At that time it was called Machipongo High School. In 1954, a new high school was built next to the old Machipongo building, which became a consolidated elementary school for the children attending elementary schools in the central part of Northampton County.[210] In time an annex was built to accomodate increasing numbers of children attending Machipongo Elementary School. After several years the old Machipongo school was demolished and the central office for Northampton County School Board was moved from Eastville to the Machipongo Elementary School.[211]

Machipongo High School

Machipongo Elementary School

Northampton County High School

MAPPSVILLE SCHOOL ELEMENTARY SITE, MAPPSVILLE

Mappsville Elementary School was the most northern Rosenwald School on the Eastern Shore of Virginia. The school had four classrooms and was built in the early 1920s. The total cost of the building was $3,000.00; the black community was required to contribute $1,200.00, the school board contributed $1,500.00, and the Rosenwald Foundation gave $300.00, the building plan, and the impetus. The building was used until 1964, after which it fell into disrepair and was torn down. The acreage is now used as a parking lot for the First Baptist Church in Mappsville.[212]

MARY NOTTINGHAM SMITH HIGH SCHOOL, ACCOMAC

Mary Nottingham Smith

In 1931, J. Edgar Thomas, Susie Wharton Thomas, and William H. Bailey sold a lot in the town of Accomac containing 0.842 of an acre to the trustees of Accomack County Colored High School Association for $750.00. The trustees: Reverend R. C. Hughes, W. J. Laws, R. H. Hall, G. W. Downing, Mary N. Smith, C. H. Ewell, and Alma Parker purchased the property and in 1932 built the first secondary school for black children in Accomack County.[213] This school was named for Mary Nottingham Smith, a trustee of the school and a person well known by all people on the Eastern Shore of Virginia. Born in Northampton County, Smith had worked in the Accomack County school system since 1921 as a Jeannes Educational Supervisor.

In 1953 a larger high school also named Mary Nottingham Smith was built on another site. The old 1932 Smith High School became T. C. Walker Elementary School.

Historical Marker

Mary Nottingham Smith High School opened in 1953

MOUNT NEBO ELEMENTARY SCHOOL, SLUTKILL

Children were already learning in this building when in 1894 Joseph H. Savage sold the property to the black trustees George Kellam, Edmond Martin, John Glen, Solomon Fosque, Charles Turner, Charles Bagwell, John T. Turner, Nathaniel Hitchison, Edward Chandler, William Turner, and Perry Fosque of the Mount Nebo Elementary School.[214] This one-room school served the children of this black community until the school was closed and the children sent to Savageville Elementary School. The Mount Nebo School building was renovated and now serves as a church hall for Mount Nebo Baptist Church.

Mount Nebo Elementary School

ONANCOCK ELEMENTARY SCHOOL

The first Onancock Elementary School was named the Armstrong School, after the Civil War general, Samuel Chapman Armstrong. Opened in 1867, this was a one-room, non-graded school with an enrollment of forty-seven students, seven of whom had been free before the Civil War. The school was sponsored by the A. M. E. Church and was not a part of the Freedmen's Bureau system.

On December 14, 1868, a Freedmen's Bureau School opened with the name Bowdoin. Phebe E. Hensen, a black woman, was the teacher. The school was an intermediate school with only ten students. Eventually the Bowdoin School replaced the Armstrong School.[215]

Onancock Elementary School

PUNGOTEAGUE ELEMENTARY SCHOOL SITE, PUNGOTEAGUE

The first school in Pungoteague opened in 1867 and was called the Smith School. It was a one room school and opened under the direction of the Freedmen's Bureau and the American Missionary Association. Its enrollment was nine-five, with sixty-five attending regularly. Of the nine-five pupils, forty-five were free before the Civil War.[216]

READTOWN ELEMENTARY SCHOOL, READTOWN

This dwelling house is the original two-room Readtown Elementary School. The lot was purchased from Peter J. Carter and his wife, Georgianna, in 1881 by black School

Readtown School

District #2.[217, 218] The irony of this purchase is that this is where the Honorable Peter J. Carter was held in slavery. The land once belonged to the Read family's plantation Jeffersonia and was left in Margaret Read's will to be sold.[219] The Readtown School was closed in 1939 when it was consolidated into the Eastville School.

The building was refurbished in the 1950s by the Jones family.

ROSENWALD SCHOOL, CAPE CHARLES

Beginning with the philosophy that "real endowments are not money but ideas" Julius Rosenwald, executive officer of Sears Roebuck & Co., the Chicago-based department store, donated money to Tuskegee Institute. By 1912 Rosenwald had given permission for Booker T. Washington to use a portion of the money to build six small schools in Alabama. The project was a success and in 1917 he set up the Julius Rosenwald Fund to dispense funds to build schools for African-American children all over the rural South. By 1928, one-fifth of all schools in the rural South for black

Julius Rosenwald
Businessman and Philanthropist

children was a Rosenwald school. By 1932 the Julius Rosenwald Fund had built 4,977 new schools. Of these, 367 were built in Virginia with a pupil capacity of 840.

One of the schools built by Rosenwald's generosity was the Cape Charles School, located "over the hump" on land acquired by the Northampton County School Board from the New York, Philadelphia and Norfolk Railroad Company in 1928.[220]

Rosenwald School in Cape Charles

W. H. Smith
First Principal of Rosenwald School

The school opened in 1936[221] and had four classrooms and an auditorium. Two of the classrooms were used for elementary children in Cape Charles and two used for secondary school pupils from all over Northampton County. William H. Smith, of Cape Charles, was the first principal. Fred Matthews drove a bus from Hare Valley to Cape Charles, picking up children all along Route 13 as he drove south. Those children living off the main highway walked out to Route 13.

When Tidewater Institute went bankrupt in the 1930s as a result of the Great Depression, Northampton County began to fund that secondary school as a part of its public system, and the Rosenwald School became an elementary school for children living in Cape Charles only. After schools were integrated, the black children attended the Cape Charles public school on Plum Street.

In 1968 Northampton County sold the school to the Robberecht Seafood Company, and for several years the building was used as a seafood processing plant.[222]

The school has been vacant since 1977 and, although in disrepair, it symbolizes an important step toward black children of the county receiving education, making it a worthy landmark.

Today, all over the South, Rosenwald Schools are being reclaimed and put to use.

T. C. Walker Consolidated Elementary School, Accomac

The T. C. Walker Elementary in Accomack was one of several schools in Virginia named for Thomas Calhoun Walker, a noted attorney from Gloucester County, Virginia. Born in slavery in 1853, he attended Hampton Institute. He became the self-appointed superintendent of Gloucester's black schools. He is noted for telling

T. C. Walker

General Samuel Chapman Armstrong at Hampton Institute *"I comes here to get some education and I ain't gonna leave till I gets some"*. He developed a closeness to the Eastern Shore through his membership and as an advisor and consultant of Negro affairs on the Virginia Emergency and Relief Administration.[223]

The T. C. Walker Consolidated Elementary School, originally the Mary Nottingham Smith High School, was renamed in 1956. The school effectively consolidated several of the small one and two room schools. An Accomack County teacher, Richard Upshur, was named the first principal of this school. After two new elementary schools, North and South Accomack Elementary Schools, were built, it became a junior high school. The school building was demolished in 1987. The land on which the school was built had been given to the county to be used for black public education. After T. C. Walker Consolidated Elementary school was razed, the land returned to the J. Edgar Thomas family.[224]

T. C. Walker Elementary School

Tidewater Institute, Cobb Station

By 1870 one- and two-room schools had been established in every town and hamlet in the Eastern Shore counties of Accomack and Northampton. Early in 1872 the new state public school system ab-sorbed the small black schools. After industrious black children worked their way through the local elementary system, they were forced to leave the Eastern Shore for further training. The peninsula needed a secondary school for black children. Following several unsuccessful attempts, the Tidewater Institute was founded by Rev. George E. Reid in 1903. Reid had served as principal of the Spiller

Tidewater Institute today

Academy in Hampton, Virginia. When the academy building burned, Reid per-suaded the Eastern Shore Baptist Sunday School Convention and the Northampton Baptist Association to take over the remains of the academy and operate it on the Eastern Shore under the name of Tidewater Institute. The stated mission of the new school was to "help to improve the industrial, intellectual, moral, and religious condition of the black youth on the Eastern Shore of Virginia. . . . [and] to prepare young men and women for life's duties, inculcate the spirit of service and inspire them to lead noble lives."

Tidewater Institute operated for two years in the Mount Maria Tent's Hall in Cheriton and in the old Union Baptist Church in Eastville. Slowly the school

Tidewater Institute

began to grow, serving children from both Northampton and Accomack counties as well as children from off the Eastern Shore. In 1908 the institute purchased two acres of land from Littleton Bibbins on what is now called Cobbs Station Road, six miles from Cape Charles and three miles from Eastville. A building was soon erected on the site. In 1914 the Tidewater board of trustees purchased another acre and a quarter of land and began work on a larger building. In 1916 the board entered into an agreement to safeguard the adjoining farm for the Institute, but not until 1925 was the land purchased. Nevertheless, a house for the principal was built on the property between 1916 and 1917. At the height of Tidewater Institute's success it owned forty-two acres on Cobbs Station Road convenient to the rail station. The physical plant included a pair of dormitories separately housing nearly one hundred boys and girls.[225]

Meanwhile, the Tidewater Institute expanded its curriculum, accommodating not only the high school but also several lower grades. By 1916 Tidewater Institute had graduated nine students, several of whom went on to higher learning and some later taught at the Institute. In 1918 Rev. U. G. Wilson replaced Rev. Reid as the principal. Under Wilson's direction the school expanded in both physical plant and curriculum. In 1919 Tidewater added a Normal Training High School Course and received from the state a charter granting full industrial, academic, collegiate, and seminary powers.

State Historic Marker

Tidewater was a Baptist school. Its principals were Baptist ministers. Sunday School and preaching services were held Sundays and prayer services were conducted by members of the faculty on Thursday evenings. Students were required to attend. The more advanced students formed a Sunday School training class.[226]

In the fall of 1927, just before the Great Depression, Rev. J. R. Custis became the new Tidewater principal. In spite of the economic crisis, Tidewater made progress for several years. During the early 1930s the high school division was accredited as a private secondary school by the State Education Office of the Commonwealth of Virginia. However, Tidewater Institute had no endowment. It was supported directly by school tuition and by funds supplied by the Eastern Shore Baptist Sunday School Convention, the Northampton Baptist Association, the Woman's Education and Missionary Circle of the Eastern Shore of Virginia, and the other affiliated Baptist organizations. It was perhaps inevitable that the down-turn in the economy would eventually affect Tidewater Institute. Even though the Institute was the only school charged with providing secondary education for black youth on the Eastern Shore of Virginia, neither the Northampton nor Accomack school systems nor the state of Virginia contributed to the operation of the institution. Faced with mounting debts, in 1935 Tidewater Institute closed its doors.[227]

In 1940 the trustees of Tidewater Institute sold the property to pay long-standing bills. Three acres and the girls' dormitory were sold to the pastor of African Baptist Church. The balance of the property was sold to Paul Bibbins, the grandson of Littleton Bibbins. The girl's dormitory became an apartment house which burned in 1953. The boy's dormitory was later remodeled and is now a private dwelling.

TIDEWATER AS A PUBLIC SCHOOL

In response to a request from the Board of Trustees of the Tidewater Institute the Northampton County School Board decided to take over the operation of the Tidewater Institute. September 18, 1935, Northampton County began using the buildings at Tidewater Institute as a high school for black children. George E. Downing, a local African-American attorney became the first principal of the school. Downing, a graduate of Virginia Union University and Boston University, served as principal until 1937.[228] Eva Ruff and Mary Hawkins, both of Virginia State College, and a Mr. Jones of Hampton Institute were the first black secondary teachers for Northampton County. The Northampton Times reported that one hundred and ninety-seven black children presented themselves on that first day. The buildings were used until 1941, when the high school was moved to an abandoned white school in Machipongo. For further discussion of this subject see Machipongo High School and Northampton County High School.[229]

TOWNSEND ELEMENTARY SCHOOL SITE, TOWNSEND, VIRGINIA

The Townsend School was opened sometime after 1912, when the School Board purchased two acres from First Baptist Church of Capeville.[230] It served the area as a school until 1946, when it was absorbed into the Capeville Consolidated Elementary School. In 1947 it was sold to Hensel D. Spady. There were no structures on this property when it was purchased by Spady.[231]

WHITESVILLE ELEMENTARY SCHOOL, WHITESVILLE

Located at the end of the Leslie Trent Road, the Whitesville Elementary School was built in the mid 1920s at a cost of $6,750.00. The contribution from the black community was $1,700.00 and $900.00 from the Rosenwald Foundation. The school served until 1964 when schools were integrated. [236] It is currently being renovated by a church group.[232]

Whitesville Elementary School a Rosenwald School

GPS Coordinates

Accomac Elementary School, Accomac	37°42.94N	075°40.66W
Adams United Methodist Church, Whitesville	37°45.90N	075°42.19W
African Baptist Church & Parsonage, Sunny Side Rd., Cheriton	37°17.26N	075°57.85W
Allen Private School, Bayside Rd., Hare Valley	37°29.75N	075°51.54W
Ames Funeral Home, Route 13, Melfa	37°39.31N	075°44.36W
Ayres/Johnson Cemetery, Morleys Wharf Rd., Wardtown	37°32.46N	075°48.95W
Bailey Cemetery, Kilmontown Rd., Melfa	37°39.64N	075°45.64W
Bayside Elementary School, Bayside Rd., Bayside	37°44.84N	075°43.10W
Belle Haven Elementary School, Big Pine Rd., Belle Haven	37°34.08N	075°48.66W
Bethany School, Washington Ave, Cape Charles	37°16.52N	075°56.96W
Bethel A. M. E. Church & Parsonage, Courthouse Rd., Eastville	37°21.84N	075°56.54W
Bethel A.M.E. Church, Boundary St, Onancock	37°42.80N	075°43.95W
Bethel Baptist Church, , Bayside Rd., Franktown	37°29.05N	075°52.09W
Bibbins Cemetery, Capt Howe Rd., Eastville	37°21.15N	075°56.78W
Boston Elementary School, Boston Rd., Boston	37°36.27N	075°50.80W
Brickhouse Banking Company, Bayside Rd., Hare Valley	37°29.83N	075°51.47W
Brickhouse Cemetery, Bayside Rd., Hare Valley	37°29.82N	075°51.46W
Brickhouse Dwelling, Bayside Rd., Hare Valley	37°30.12N	075°51.22W
Bridgetown School, Bayside Rd., Bridgetown	37°26.67N	075°55.63W
Burris Graveyard and Home, Cherry Dale Rd., Eastville	37°22.32N	075°55.51W
Burton's Chapel Indept. Methodist Church, Burton's Chapel Rd.	37°38.23N	075°42.27W
Burton's Elementary School, Burton's Chapel Rd.,	37°38.24N	075°42.28W

Capeville Consolidated Elementary School, Rte 600, Capeville	37°11.94N	075°57.58W
Carter Cemetery, , Bayside Rd., Franktown	37°28.59N	075°53.11W
Carver Movie House, Cape Charles	37°16.38N	076°01.00W
Cheapside Elementary School, Arlington Rd., Cheapside	37°12.06N	075°59.04W
Cheriton Elementary School, Cherrystone	37°17.99N	075°59.99W
Cheriton Grammar School, Sunny Side Rd., Cheriton	37°17.32N	075°57.29W
Cherrystone Baptist Church, Cherrystone	37°17.99N	075°59.70W
Craddockville School, Craddockville Rd., Craddockville	37°34.26N	075°52.65W
Dalby's School Site, Plantation Station Rd., Dalby	37°14.52N	075°57.24W
Daugherty Elementary School, Drummondtown Rd., Daugherty	37°41.08N	075°39.87W
Deas Chapel United Methodist Church, Horntown Rd., Horntown	37°58.89N	075°27.21W
Eastville Elementary School, Church Rd., Eastville	37°21.88N	075°56.38W
Eastville Elementary School, James Circle, Eastville	37°21.86N	075°56.42W
Ebenezar A. M. E. Church & Parsonage, Cheapside	37°12.68N	075°58.64W
Ebenezer Baptist Church, Occohonnock Neck Rd., Wardtown	37°32.16N	075°51.68W
Exmore Elementary School, Occohonnock Neck Rd., Exmore	37°32.14N	075°49.82W
First Baptist Church Old Parsonage, Cheapside	37°12.21N	075°58.63W
First Baptist Church Parsonage, Route 13, Capeville	37°13.90N	075°58.25W
First Baptist Church Sexton House, Route 13, Capeville	37°13.89N	075°58.25W
First Baptist Church, Cape Charles	37°16.32N	076°00.73W
First Baptist Church, Route 13, Capeville	37°13.94N	075°58.22W
First Baptist Church, Seaside Rd., Mappsville	37°50.32N	075°32.74W
Floyd Restaurant, Route 13, Melfa	37°38.15N	075°45.12W

Franktown Elemenatry School, Bayside Rd., Franktown	37°28.55N	075°53.16W
Friendship United Methodist Church, Wattsville	37°56.08N	075°30.43W
Gaskins Chapel A. M. E. Church, Savageville Rd., Savageville	37°41.00N	075°45.26W
Gaskins Chapel A. M. E., Kitten Branch Rd, Savageville	37°41.11N	075°45.23W
Grace Independent Methodist Church, Wachapreague	37°36.60N	075°41.96W
Grand Army of the Republic, Old Town Neck Rd., Eastville	37°21.88N	075°56.38W
Gray's Funeral Home, Jefferson Ave, Cape Charles	37°16.32N	076°00.97W
Gray's Funeral Home, Randolph Ave, Cape Charles	37°16.27N	076°00.79W
Gunter Funeral Home, Market Street, Onancock	37°42.38N	075°43.85W
Hare Valley Elementary School, Bayside Rd, Hare Valley	37°30.20N	075°51.18W
Hare Valley Elementary School, First, Bayside Rd, Hare Valley	37°30.81N	075°55.78W
Hare Valley Elementary School, Newest, Bayside Rd, Hare Valley	37°30.65N	075°50.69W
Holland's Funeral Home, Bayside Rd, Hare Valley	37°30.20N	075°51.18W
Holland's Funeral Home, Business 13, Cheriton	37°17.24N	075°57.94W
Holland's Funeral Home, Sunny Side Rd, Cheriton	37°17.30N	075.57.31W
Hopeville Mission, Route 600, Cedar Grove	37°09.87N	075°57.95W
Jamesville Elementary School, Saltworks Rd, Jamesville	37°30.89N	075°55.94W
Jefferson Grocery Store, Mason Ave, Cape Charles	37°16.09N	076°00.71W
Jefferson Grocery Store, Mason Ave, Cape Charles	37°16.11N	076°00.68W
Jerusalem Baptist Church, Termperanceville	37°54.21N	075°32.57W
Lone Star Masonic Lodge #38, Old Stage Rd, Pungoteague	37°38.02N	075°48.58W
Macedonia A. M. E. Church, Church Rd, Accomac	37°42.85N	075°40.71W
Macedonia Elementary School, Accomac	37°49.21N	075°38.98W
Macedonia Masonic Lodge #19, Church Rd, Accomac	37°42.88N	075°40.69W

Machipongo Elementary School, Machipongo	37°25.58N	075°53.47W
Mallie Movie House, Route 13, Treherneville	37°25.70N	075°53.51W
Mapp Cemetery, Route 600, Cobb Station	37°18.49N	075°56.03W
Mappsville Elementary School, Seaside Rd, Mappsville	37°50.31N	075°32.84W
Mary Nottingham Smith High School, Front St, Accomac	37°42.98N	075°40.66W
Mary Nottingham Smith High School, M. N. Smith Rd, Accomac	37°44.23N	075°38.98W
Metompkin Baptist Church, Route 13, Parksley	37°45.51N	075°37.10W
Metropolitan Memorial United Methodist Church, Bayside Rd, Bayside	37°44.84N	075°43.09W
Mitchell's Store, Jefferson Ave, Cape Charles	37°16.32N	076°01.05W
Morris Funeral Home & Morris Store, Arlington Rd, Cheapside	37°11.58N	075°58.95W
Morris Funeral Home, Nassawadox, Route 13, Nassawadox	37°29.61N	075°51.67W
Mount Nebo Baptist Church & Mount Nebo School, Omega Rd, Slutkill	37°40.59N	075°48.12W
Mount Olive Baptist Church, Hacks Neck Rd, Hacks Neck	37°39.09N	075°50.69W
Mount Olive Baptist Church, Jenkins Bridge	37°55.46N	075°37.62W
Mount Zion A. M. E. Battle Point Rd, Jamesville	37°32.08N	075°48.41W
Mount Zion A. M. E. Treherneville	37°25.70N	075°53.52W
Mount Zion Royal #8, Treherneville	37°26.43N	075°55.43W
Mystic Masonic Lodge, Savageville Rd, Savageville	37°41.02N	075°45.23W
Nassawadox Elementary School	37°28.44N	075°53.30W
New Allen A. M. E. Church, Bayside Rd, Franktown	37°29.39N	075°50.93W
New Mount Calvary Baptist Church, Seaside Rd, Exmore	37°32.13N	075°49.82W
New Mount. Zion Baptist Church & Elementary School, Coal Kiln Rd	37°33.94N	075°46.63W
Odd Fellows Lodge Hall #2774, Courthouse Rd, Eastville	37°21.80N	075°56.46W

Odd Fellows Lodge Hall #3233, Courthouse Rd, Eastville	37°21.81N	075°56.43W
Onancock Elementary School, Boundary St, Onancock	37°42.69N	075°43.98W
Outlaw Black Smithshop, Boundary St, Onancock	37°42.61N	075°05.13W
Palm Tavern, Mason Ave, Cape Charles	37°16.03N	076-01.00W
Pitts Movie House, Boundary St, Onancock	37°42.69N	075°44.01W
Pride of Virginia Masonic Lodge #18, Courthouse Rd, Eastville	37°22.01N	075°55.63W
Pungoteague Elementary School, Old Stage Rd, Pungoteague	37°38.03N	075°48.37W.
Read House, Bayside Rd, Hare Valley	37°29.80N	075°51.46W
Readtown Elementary School, Bell Lane, Readtown	37°24.21N	075°54.60W
Rosenwald School, Cape Charles	37°15.81N	076°00.57W
Saint John Baptist Church, Church St, Onancock	37°42.84N	075°44.11W
Saint John United Methodist Church, Messongo	37°55.50N	075°37.79W
Saint Joseph A. M. E. Church, Big Pine Rd, Belle Haven	37°34.03N	075°48.66W
Saint Luke A. M. E. Church, Drummondtown Rd, Daugherty	37°41.08N	075°39.87W
Saint Paul A. M. E. Church, Old Stage Rd, Pungoteague	37°38.03N	075°48.58W
Saint Stephens A.M.E. Church, Cape Charles	37°16.33N	076°00.90W
Sample Barber Shop, Jefferson Ave, Cape Charles	37°16.33N	076°00.89W
Saunders Funeral Home, Culls	37°17.07N	075°58.24W
Saunders/Baker Cemetery, Culls	37°16.75N	075°58.03W
Shiloh Baptist Church, Boston Rd, Boston	37°36.68N	075°50.40W
Shorter's Chapel A.M.E., Bayside Rd, Bridgetownn	37°27.81N	075°53.30W
Snead's United Methodist Church, Seaside Rd,	37°35.53N	075°45.17W
Spence's Methodist Church, Route 13, Exmore	37°32.46N	075°48.95W
Susan Riley House, Bayside Rd, Bayside Rd, Bayside	37°44.92N	075°43.05W

T. C. Walker Elementary School, Front St, Accomac	37°42.98N	075°40.66W
Tabernacle Baptist Church, Flemming Rd, Horntown	37°57.95N	075°28.05W
Tasley Fairground, Fairground Rd, Tasley	37°42.55N	075°42.66W
Thomas Funeral Home, Edgar Thomas Rd, Accomac	37°42.95N	075°41.65W
Tidewater Institute, Cobbs Station Rd, Cobbs Station	37°18.45N	075°56.90W
Townsend Elementary School, Arlington Rd, Cheapside	37°11.07N	075°58.66W
Trent Grocery Store, Whitesville	37°46.84N	075°39.67W
Union Baptist Church, Route 13, Eastville	37°23.02N	075°54.95W
Upshur Blacksmith Shop, Nassawadox	37°28.27N	075°51.66W
Upshur Service Grocery Store & Beauty Salon, Route 13, Nassawadox	37°29.43N	075°50.91W
Upshur Service Station and Store, Route 13, Nassawadox	37°28.27N	075°51.85W
Weirwood Fairgrounds, Weirwood	37°28.24N	075°51.70W
Wharton Building, Front St & Church Rd, Accomac	37°42.97N	075°40.58W
Whitesville Elementary School, Whitesville	37°46.96N	075°39.79W
Wright's Blacksmith Shop, Old Town Neck Rd, Eastville	37°21.91N	075°56.13W

Map Locations

NORTHAMPTON

1. Hopeville Mission, Route 600, Cedar Grove.
2. Townsend Elementary School, Arlington Road, Cheapside.
3. Morris Funeral Home & Morris Store, Arlington Road, Cheapside.
4. Capeville Consolidated Elementary School, Route 600, Capeville.
5. Cheapside Elementary School, Arlington Road, Cheapside.
6. First Baptist Church Old Parsonage, Cheapside
7. Ebenezar A. M. E. Church & Parsonage, Cheapside.
8. First Baptist Church Sexton House, Route 13, Capeville.
9. First Baptist Church Parsonage, Route 13, Capeville.
10. First Baptist Church, Route 13, Capeville.
11. Dalby's School Site, Plantation Station Road, Dalby.
12. Rosenwald School, Old Road, Cape Charles.
13. Jefferson Grocery Store, Mason Avenue, Cape Charles.
14. Palm Tavern, Mason Avenue, Cape Charles.
15. Gray's Funeral Home, Randolph Ave, Cape Charles.
16. Gray's Funeral Home, Jefferson Ave, Cape Charles.
17. Saint Stephens A.M.E. Church, Cape Charles.
18. First Baptist Church, Cape Charles.
19. Bethany School, Washington Avenue, Cape Charles.
20. Sample Barber Shop, Cape Charles.
21. Mitchell's Store, Cape Charles.
22. Carver Movie House, Cape Charles.
23. Saunders Funeral Home, Culls Road, Culls.
24. Saunders/Baker Cemetery, Culls Road, Culls.
25. Holland's Funeral Home, Business 13, Cheriton.
26. African Baptist Church & Parsonage, Sunny Side Road, Cheriton .
27. Holland's Funeral Home, Sunny Side Road, Cheriton.

28. Cheriton Grammar School, Sunny Side Road, Cheriton.

29. Cheriton Elementary School, Huntingtom Farm, Cherrystone.

30. Cherrystone Baptist Church, Cherrystone.

31. Tidewater Institute, Cobbs Station Road, Cobbs Station.

32. Mapp Cemetery, Route 600, Cobb Station.

33. Bibbins Cemetery, Capt Howe Road, Eastville.

34. Odd Fellows Lodge Hall #2774, Courthouse Road, Eastville.

35. Odd Fellows Lodge Hall #3233, Courthouse Road, Eastville.

36. Bethel A. M. E. Church & Parsonage, Courthouse Road, Eastville.

37. Eastville Elementary School, James Circle, Eastville.

38. Eastville Elementary School, Church Road, Eastville.

39. Grand Army of the Republic, Old Town Neck Road, Eastville.

40. Wright's Blacksmith Shop, Old Town Neck Road, Eastville.

41. Pride of Virginia Masonic Lodge #18, Courthouse Road, Eastville .

42. Burris Graveyard and Home, Cherry Dale Road, Eastville.

43. Union Baptist Church, Route 13, Eastville.

44. Readtown Elementary School, Bell Lane, Readtown.

45. Machipongo Elementary School, Young Street, Machipongo.

46. Mallie Movie House Route 13, Treherneville.

47. Mount Zion A. M. E. Church, Treherneville Drive, Treherneville.

48. Mount Zion Royal #8, Treherneville Drive, Treherneville.

49. Bridgetown School, Bayside Road, Bridgetown.

50. Shorter's Chapel A.M.E., Bayside Road, Bridgetown.

51. Weirwood Fairgrounds, Bayford Road, Weirwood.

52. Upshur Blacksmith Shop, Franktown Road, Nassawadox.

53. Upshur Service Station and Store, Route 13, Nassawadox.

54. Nassawadox Elementary School, Franktown Road, Nassawadox.

55. Franktown Elemenatry School, Bayside Road, Franktown.

56. Carter Cemetery Bayside Road, Franktown.

57. Bethel Baptist Church, Bayside Road, Franktown.

58. New Allen A. M. E. Church, Bayside Road, Franktown.

59. Upshur Service Grocery Store & Beauty Salon, Route 13, Nassawadox.

60. Morris Funeral Home, Route 13, Nassawadox.

61. Allen Private School, Bayside Road, Hare Valley.

62. Read House, Bayside Road, Hare Valley.

63. Brickhouse CemeteryBayside Road, Hare Valley.

64. Brickhouse Banking Company, Bayside Road, Hare Valley.

65. Brickhouse Dwelling, Bayside Road, Hare Valley.

66. Holland's Funeral Home, Bayside Road, Hare Valley.

67. Hare Valley Elementary School, First, Bayside Road, Hare Valley.

68. Hare Valley Elementary School, Newest, Bayside Road, Hare Valley.

69. Hare Valley Elementary School, Bayside Road, Hare Valley.

70. Jamesville Elementary School, Saltworks Road, Jamesville.

71. Mount Zion A. M. E. Church, Battle Point Road, Jamesville

72. Ayres/Johnson Cemetery, Morleys Wharf Road, Wardtown.

73. Ebenezer Baptist Church, Occahonnack Neck Road, Wardtown

74. Exmore Elementary School, Occahonnack Neck Road, Exmore.

75. Spence's Methodist Church, Route 13, Exmore.

76. New Mount Calvary Baptist Church, Seaside Road, Exmore.

ACCOMACK

1. New Mount. Zion Baptist Church & Elementary School, Coal Kiln Road

2. Craddockville Elementary School

3. Saint Joseph A. M. E. Church

4. Belle Haven Elementary School

5. Snead's United Methodist Church

6. Boston Elementary School

7. Grace Independent Methodist Church

8. Shiloh Baptist Church

9. Lone Star Masonic Lodge #38

10. Saint Paul A. M. E. Church, Pungoteague

11. Pungoteague Elementary School

12. Floyd Restaurant, Route 13, Melfa

13. Burton's Chapel Independent Methodist Church

14. Burton's Elementary School

15.   Mount Olive Baptist Church, Hacks Neck Road, Hacks Neck.

16.   Ames Funeral Home, Route 13, Melfa.

17.   Bailey Cemetery, Kilmontown Road, Melfa.

18.   Mount Nebo Church and School, Omega Road, Slutkill Neck

19   Gaskins Chapel A. M. E. Church, Savageville Road, Savageville

20.   Mystic Masonic Lodge, Savageville Road, Savageville

21.   Daugherty Elementary School, Drummondtown Road, Daugherty

22.   Saint Luke A. M. E. Church, Drummondtown Road, Daugherty

23.   Gaskins Chapel A. M. E., Kitten Branch Rd

24.   Gunter Funeral Home, Market Street, Onancockk

25.   Tasley Fairground, Fairground Road, Tasley

26.   Outlaw Black Smithshop, Boundary Street, Onancock

27.   Pitts Movie House, Boundary Street, Onancock

28.   Onancock Elementary School, Boundary Street, Onancock

29.   Bethel A.M.E. Church, Boundary Street, Onancock

30.   Saint John Baptist Church, Church Street, Onancock

31.   Macedonia A. M. E. Church, Church Road, Accomac

32.   Macedonia Masonic Lodge #19, Church Road, Accomac

33.   Accomac Elementary School, Accomac

34.   Thomas Funeral Home, Accomac

35.   Wharton Building, Accomac

36.   Mary Nottingham Smith High School/T. C. Walker School, Accomac

37.   Mary Nottingham Smith High School, Route 13, Acomac

38.   Metropolitan Memorial United Methodist Church, Bayside Road, Baysid

39.   Bayside Elementary School, Bayside Road, Bayside

40.   Susan Riley House, Bayside Road, Bayside Road, Bayside

41.   Metompkin Baptist Church, Route 13, Parksley

42.   Adams United Methodist Church, Whitesville

43.   Trent Grocery Store, Whitesville

44.   Whitesville Elementary School, Whitesville

45.   Macedonia Elementary School, Accomac

46.   Mappsville Elementary School, Mappsville

47.   First Baptist Church, Mappsville

48. Jerusalem Baptist Church, Termperanceville

49. Mount Olive Baptist Church, Jenkins Bridge

50. Friendship United Methodist Church, Wattsville

51. Saint John United Methodist Church, Messongo

52. Tabernacle Baptist Church, Horntown

53. Deas Chapel United Methodist Church, Horntown

End Notes

BUSINESSES

1.   Freedmen's Bureau Records Microfilm.

2.   Payne, Daniel Alexander, *Recollections of Seventy Years*, A. M. E. Sunday School Union, 1888 Nashville, Tenn.

3.   Interviewed Dorothy Riley White.

4.   Eastern Shore News

5.   Miles, Barry & M. K. Miles, *Marriage Records of Accomack Count, Va., 1854-1895*, Heritage Books.

6.   Barnes, Brooks Miles, "Onancock Race Riot of 1907," *Virginia Magazine of History of Biography 92 (July, 1984), 336-351.*

7.   Nock, L. Floyd, *What the Saturday Evening Post Missed, Accomac, Virginia.*

8.   Northampton County Charter Book 1, p. 127.

9.   Northampton County Charter Book 1, p. 152.

10. Interviewed Edgar Wharton.

11. Northampton County Charter Book No. 2, p. 9.

12. Northampton County Deed Book No. 65, p. 122.

13. Interviewed Calvin Brickhouse.

14. Northampton County Charter Book No. 3,p. 381.

15. Northampton Times, 30 May 1940.

16. Northampton Times, 4 April 1940.

17. Northampton Times, 11 Sept 1947.

18. Eastern Shore News, 29 March 1946.

19. Interviewed George Floyd, Vernice Willis and Elizabeth Bagwell.

20. Northampton Times, 1934.

21. Interviewed Thomas G. Godwin

22. Interviewed Greta Taylor.

23. Northampton County Deed Book No. 94, p. 373.

24. Northampton County Deed Book No. 95, p. 105.

25. Northampton County Deed Book No. 122, p. 440.

26. Interviewed Mignon Holland Anderson and Mathew Cornish, Jr., 2006.

27. Northampton Times: 6 August 1936.

28. Northampton County Deed Book No. 88, p. 248.

29. Interviewed Arthur Carter and Calvin Brickhouse, 2006.

30. Federal Census 1920, Capeville District p. 7.

31. Interviews: Lenore Mitchell, David Mitchell, and Mabel Mitchell.

32. Morris Family Records.

33. Interviewed Alvin Morris, Eunice Morris.

34. 1920 United States Census.

35. Interviewed John Verrill, Jan. 2006.

36. Latimer, Frances B., *Cape Charles: A Place for all People*, Hickory House, Eastville, Va,1996.

37. Eastern Shore News: Restaurant Razed 1993.

38. Interviewed Jesse Poulson and Marie Humbles.

39. Northampton County Medical Register p. 1.

40. Northampton County Deed Book No. 72, p. 277.

41. Northampton County Medical Register, p. 25.

42. Northampton County Medical Register, p. 29.

43. Northampton County Marriage Records.

44. Northampton Times, 4 May 1939.

45. Interviewed Willie Collins and Brenda Sample Williams, June 2006.

46. Northampton County Deed Book No. 42, p. 295.

47. Interviewed Henry Baker.

48. Peninsula Enterprise, Aug. 1902.

49. Eastern Shore News, Aug. 1902.

50. Interviewed Marie Humbles.

51. Northampton County Charter Book No. 3, p.41.

52. Northampton County Deed Book No. 82, p.462

53. Weirwood Fair Souvenir Booklet, 1955.

54. Eastern Shore News, Feb. 1961.

55. Interviewed Marie Humbles.

56. Interviewed Thomas Trent, May 2006.

57. Interviewed Paul E. Bibbins.

58. Interviewed Lucille Upshur Kornegay. Upshur Stores

59. Accomack County Deed Book No.

60. Interviewed Edgar Wharton, July 2006.

61. Interviewed Carolyn Wright Arnell, Nov. 2006.

CEMETERY

62. Accomack County Deed Book No. No. 86, p. 539.

63. Interviewed Lucy Bailey Smith.

64. Northampton County Deed Book No. 34, p. 65.

65. Interviewed Paul Bibbins.

66. Northampton County Deed Book No. 44, p.346.

67. Interviewed Calvin Brickhouse.

68. Northampton County Deed Book No. 36, p. 691.

69. Interviewed Eugenia Burris Fox.

70. Northampton County Deed Book No. 39, p. 535.

71. Interviewed Arthur T. Carter, Aug. 2006.

72. Accomack County Order Book 1804-1805, p. 194.

73. Northampton County Deed Book No. 38, p. 381.

74. Interviewed George Ayers.

75. Northampton County Deed Book No. 55, p.203.

76. Interviewed Alvin Mapp.

77. Northampton County Deed Book No.38, p. 304.

78. Interviewed Henry Baker.

CHURCHES

79. Old Adams Methodist Church History

80. Old Adams Methodist Church History

81. Northampton County Deed Book No. 37, p.297

82. Northampton County Deed Book No. 45, p. 445.

83. African Baptist Church History.

84. Bethel A. M. E. Church History.

85. Northampton County Deed Book No. 37, p. 207.

86. Bethel A. M. E. Church History.

87. Accomack County Deed Book No. ,

88. Accomack County Deed Book No.,

89.   Northampton County Deed Book No. 52, p. 25.

90.   Bethel Baptist Church History.

91.   Interviewed Calvin Brickhouse, June 2006.

92.   Accomack County Deed Book No. 72, p. 88.

93.   Burton's Chapel Independent Methodist Church History.

94.   Phyllis Mears, Burton's Chapel.

95.   Northampton County Deed Book No. 39, p. 659.

96.   Interviewed Ronnie Holden, August 2006.

97.   Mears, James E., *Virginia's Eastern Shore in the War of Secession and in the Reconstruction Period* (22-R).

98.   Accomack County Deed Book No. 69, p. 574.

99.   Accomack County Deed Book No. 50, p. 617.

100.   Accomack County Deed Book No. 57, pp. 504-505.

101.   Deas Chapel Church History.

102.   Northampton County Deed Book No. 38, p. 650.

103.   Ebenezer A. M. E. Church History.

104.   Ebenezer Baptist Church Old History.

105.   Northampton County Deed Book No. 77, p. 342.

106.   Northampton County Deed Book No. 81, p. 46.

107.   Northampton County Deed Book No. First Baptist Church in Capeville,

108.   First Baptist in Capeville Church History

109.   Northampton County Deed Book No.

110.   First Baptist Church of Mappsville History.

111.   Accomack County Deed Book No. 67. p. 255.

112.   Interview Rudolph Tull, Aug. 2006.

113.   Wayman, Rev. A. W., *My Recollections of African M. E. Ministers, or Forty Years' Experience in the African Methodist Episcopal Church A. M. E.* Book Rooms, 631 Pine Street, 1881.

114.   Accomack County Deed Book No. 74, p. 564. Gaskins Chapel A. M. E.

115.   Accomack County Deed Book No. 78, p. 556. Gaskins Chapel A. M. E.

116.   Grace Independent Methodist Church History.

117.   Accomack County Deed Book No. 51, p. 609.

118.   Jerusalem Baptist Church History.

119.   Interviewed LaRue Holden and Ronnie Holden.

120.   Butt, Rev. Israel L., *History of African Methodism in Virginia or Four Decades in the Old Dominion*, Hampton Institute Press, Hampton, Va, 1908.

121.   Accomack County Deed Book No. 61, p. 279.

122.   Interviewed Regina Finney, June 2006.

123.   Baptist Association Souvenir Book, 1967.

124.   Metompkin Baptist Church History.

125.   Interviewed Arline Purnell, May 2006.

126.   Accomack County Deed Book No. 72, p. 65.

127.   Metropolitan Memorial Methodist Church History.

128.   Accomack County Deed Book No. 57, p. 403.

129.   Baptist Association Souvenir Book, 1967.

130.   Accomack County Deed Book No. 71, 598.

131.   Baptist Association Souvenir Book, 1967.

132.   Interviewed Marion Sample, June 2006.

133.   Accomack County Deed Book No. 60, p.15.

134.   Accomack County Deed Book No. 124, p. 600.

135.   Northampton County Deed Book No. 37, p. 472.

136.   Northampton County Deed Book No. Mount Zion A. M. E., Treherne

137.   Northampton County Deed Book No. 37, p. 658.

138.   New Allen A. M. E. Church History.

139.   New Mount Calvary Baptist Church History.

140.   Baptist Association Souvenir Book, 1967.

141.   Interviewed Oliver Custis.

142.   Saint Joseph A. M. E. Church Cornerstone.

143.   Accomack County Deed Book No. 56, p. 750.

144.   Shiloh Baptist Church History.

145.   Accomack County Deed Book No. 59, p.233.

146.   Accomack County Deed Book No. 87, p. 375.

147.   Accomack County Deed Book No. 124, p. 600.

148.   St. Luke A. M. E. Church History.

149.   Interviewed Jack Johnson, Aug. 2006.

150.   Northampton County Chancery Book No. 7, p. 195.

151.   Northampton County Deed Book No. 52, p. 374.

152.   Northampton County Deed Book No. 67, p. 230.

153.   Northampton County Deed Book No. 48, p. 410.

154.   Accomack County Deed Book No. 55, p. 92.

155. Accomack County Deed Book No., 160, p. 218.

156. Spence Chapel Methodist Church History.

157. Accomack County Deed Book No. 90, p. 110.

158. Union Baptist Church History.

159. Baptist Association Souvenir Book, 1967.

LODGES

160 Northampton County Deed Book No. 44, p. 569.

161. Northampton County Deed Book No. 101, p. 414.

162. Accomack County Deed Book No. No. No. 78, p.128.

163. Northampton County Deed Book No. 49, p.443.

164. Northampton County Deed Book No. 42, p. 664.

165. Accomack County Deed Book No. 55, p. 191.

166. Northampton County Deed Book No. 68, p. 222.

167. Accomack County Deed Book No. 86, p. 382.

SCHOOLS

168. Accomack County Deed Book No. 116, p. 528-530.

169. Northampton County Deed Book No. 96, p. 2.

170. Interviewed Lucille Upshur Kornegay, attendee of the school.

171. Interviewed Jesse Poulson.

172. Accomack County Deed Book No. No. 103, p. 251.

173. Northampton County Deed Book No. 47, p. 257-258.

174. Northampton County Deed Book No. 47, p. 267.

175. Northampton County Deed Book No. 47, p. 268.

176. Interviewed Mabel Mitchell and David Mitchell, June 2006.

177. Freedmen's Bureau Records, Microfilm.

178. www.rosenwaldschools.com/history.html.

179. Northampton County Deed Book No. 48, p. 410.

180. Interviewed Paul E. Bibbins and Viola Poole.

181. Northampton County Deed Book 128, p. 89.

182. Eastern Shore Educator.

183. Interviewed Phyllis Mears, July 2006.

184. Northampton County Deed Book No. 76, p. 78.

185. Northampton Times, Sept 5, 1946.

186. Eastern Shore Educator.

187. Northampton County Deed Book No. 111, p. 287.

188. Northampton County Deed Book No. 49, p. 61.

189. Eastern Shore News, April 12, 1946.

190. Northampton County Deed Book No. 111, p. 272.

191. Northampton County Deed Book No. 48, p. 162.

192. Accomack County Deed Book No. 104, p. 161.

193. Northampton County Deed Book No. 111, p. 286.

194. Northampton County Deed Book No. 112, p. 380.

195. Interviewed James E. Braxton and Mable Owens.

196. Interviewed Irvin Jarvis.

197. Interviewed Irvin Jarvis.

198. Northampton County Deed Book No.73, p.204.

199. Northampton County Deed Book 75, p. 227.

200. Interviewed James Kellam.

201. Freedmen's Bureau Records, Microfilm.

202. Northampton County Deed Book No. 63, p. 301.

203. Interviewed Calvin Brickhouse and Lucille Upshur Kornegay.

204. Northampton County Deed Book No. 116, p. 314.

205. Northampton County Deed Book No. 71, p. 203.

206. Accomack County Deed Book No. 68, p. 428.

207. Northampton County Deed Book No. 111, p. 294.

208. Accomack County Deed Book No. 205, p. 238.

209. Northampton County Deed Book No. 76, p. 586.

210. Northampton County Deed Book No. 126, p. 122.

211. Northampton County Deed Book No. 151, p. 295.

212. http://www.rosenwaldschools.com/history.html.

213. Accomack County Deed Book No. 141, p. 115.

214. Accomack County Deed Book No. 66, p. 591.

215. Freedmen's Bureau Records, Microfilm.

216. Freedmen's Bureau Records, Microfilm.

217. Northampton County Deed Book No. 40, p. 493.

218. Northampton County Deed Book No. 101, p. 252.

219. Northampton County Will Book No. 139, p. 151.

220. Northampton County Deed Book No. 131, p. 134.

221. Although it is commonly thought that the Rosenwald School in Cape Charles opened in 1936, according to an interview with Conway Downing, June 2004, the school opened in 1930 and George E. Downing, a local attorney, was the first principal. William H. Smith became principal in 1936.

222. Northampton County Deed Book No. 161, p. 231.

223. http://www.gloucesterva.info/history/TCWALKER.HTM.

224. Interviewed Jesse Poulson, July 2006.

225. Northampton County Deed Book No. 73, p. 18.

226. Interviewed Paul Bibbins, Frances P. Bibbins, Lillie S. Bibbins, Henry Wise, Ida Williams, and Irene Patterson.

227. Peninsula Enterprise: 7 Sept 1935.

228. Peninsula Enterprise: 7 Sept 1935

229. Northampton Times: 5 Sept 1935.

230. Northampton County Deed Book No. 66, p. 494.

231. Interviewed Denard Spady and John W. Nottingham 2006.

232. http://www.rosenwaldschools.com/history.html.

Bibliography

Baptist Association Souvenir Book, 1967.

Barnes, Brooks Miles, "Onancock Race Riot of 1907," *Virginia Magazine of History of Biography 92 (July, 1984), 336-351.*

Bently, George R., *A History of the Freedmen's Bureau.* Philadelphia: University of Pennsylvania, 1955.

Berlin, Ira. *Slaves No More.* New York, NY: Cambridge University Press, 1992.

Butt, Rev. Israel L., *History of African Methodism in Virginia or Four Decades in the Old Dominion,* Hampton Institute Press, Hampton, Va, 1908.

June Purcell Guild, *Black Laws of Virginia,* Whittet & Shepperson, 1936.

Latimer, Frances B., *Cape Charles: A Place for all People,* Hickory House, Eastville, Va, 1996.

_____, *Eastville at a Glance,* Hickory House, Eastville, Va, 2004.

Lewis, Jim, *Cape Charles: A Railroad Town,* Hickory House, Eastville, Va, 2004.

Mariner, Kirk, *Revival's Children,* Peninsula Press, Salisbury, Md, 1979.

Mears, James Egbert, *Hacks Neck and Its People,* Self Published.

Mears, James E., *Virginia's Eastern Shore in the War of Secession and in the Reconstruction Period* (22-R)

Mihalyka, Jean M., *Gravestone Inscriptions in Accomack County, Va,* Heritage Books, Inc., Bowie, Maryland.

_____, *Gravestone Inscriptions in Northampton County, Va,* Virginia State Library, Richmond, Va, 1984.

_____, *Northampton County Marriage Records, 1661-1854,* Heritage Books, Inc., Bowie, Maryland.

Miles, Barry & M. K. Miles, *Marriage Records of Accomack Count, Va., 1854-1895,* Heritage Books, Bowie, Md., 1997.

Nock, L. Floyd III, *Drummondtown, A One Horse Town,* McClure Press, 1976.

_____ , *What the Saturday Evening Post Missed, Accomac, Virginia.*

_____ , *Walking Tours of Accomac,* Dietz Press, 1986.

Payne, Daniel Alexander, *Recollections of Seventy Years,* A. M. E. Sunday School Union, 1888 Nashville, Tenn.

_____, *History of the African Methodist Episcopal Church,* A. M. E. Sunday School Union, 1891 Nashville, Tenn.

_____, *A History of the African Methodist Episcopal Church being a Volume Supplemental to a History of the African Methodist Episcopal Church*. Book Concern of the A. M. E. Church, 631 Pine Street, Philadelphia, 1922.

Schomburg, Arthur Alfonso, *The Negro Digs Up His Past*, The Survey Graphic Harlem Number, March 1925.

_____, *The Legacy of Arthur Alfonso Schomburg: A Celebration of the Past, a Vision for the Future*, The New York Public Library, 1986.

Wayman, Alexander W., *My Recollections of African M. E. Ministers, or Forty Years' Experience in the African Methodist Episcopal Church* A. M. E. Book Rooms, 631 Pine Street, 1881.

_____, *Cyclopedia of African Methodism, Methodist Episcopal Book Depository*, 108 W. Baltimore, 1882.

Williams, Ida J., *The History of Virginia State Federation of Colored Women's Clubs, Inc.*, Hickory House, 1996.

Wise, Henry A., *Over on the Eastern Shore*, Eastern Shore News, 1962.

Woodson, Carter G., *The History of the Negro Church*, Second Edition. Washington D. C., The Associated Publishers 1921.

www.gloucesterva.info/history/TCWALKER.HTM.

www.rosenwaldschools.com/history.html.

UNPUBLISHED MANUSCRIPTS

Church History of Shiloh Baptist Church, unpublished.

Church history of Jerusalem Baptist Church, unpublished.

Church history of Bethel A. M. E. Church, unpublished.

Church history of Union Baptist Church, unpublished.

Church History of New Mount Calvary Baptist Church, unpublished.

Church History of New Allen Memorial A. M. E. Church, unpublished.

Church History of First Baptist Church of Cape Charles, unpublished.

Church History of First Baptist Church of Capeville, unpublished.

Church History of Ebenezer Baptist Church, unpublished.

Church History of Metompkins Baptist Church, unpublished.

Church History of Adams United Methodist Church, unpublished.

Church History of Bethel A. M. E. Church, unpublished.

Church History of Bethel Baptist Church, unpublished.

Church History of Burton Chapel Independent Methodist Church, unpublished.

Church History of Deas Chapel Methodist Church, unpublished.

Church History of Gaskins Chapel A. M. E., unpublished.

Church History of Grace Independent Methodist Church, unpublished.

Church History of Saint Paul A. M. E. Church, unpublished.

Church History of Saint Stephens A. M. E. Church, unpublished.

Church History of Shiloh Baptist Church, unpublished.

Church History of Snead's Memorial United Methodist, unpublished.

Church History of St. John Baptist Church, unpublished.

Church History of St. John's Methodist, unpublished.

Church History of St. Luke A. M. E. Church, unpublished.

The Official Journal of the Seventy-First Annual Session of the Eastern Shore Virginia-Maryland Baptist Association and its Allied Bodies. 1955.

Minutes of the Eastern Shore Baptist Sunday School Convention, 1941.

American Missionary Society Records, unpublished.

NEWSPAPERS

Accomac News, Accomac, Virginia.

Eastern Shore Herald, Eastville, Virginia.

Eastern Shore News, Onancock, Virginia.

Eastern Virginia, Onancock, Virginia.

Headlight, Cape Charles, Virginia.

Peninsula Enterprise, Accomac, Virginia.

Pioneer, Cape Charles, Virginia.

Northampton Time, Cape Charles, Virginia.

The Eastern Shore Educator.

COURT RECORDS

Northampton County, Virginia, Charter Book, Vol. 1.

Northampton County, Virginia, Charter Book, Vol. 3.

Northampton County, Virginia, Deed Books.

Northampton County, Virginia, Death Records, 1853-1896.

Northampton County, Virginia, Birth Records, 1853-1896.

Northampton County, Virginia, Death Records 1912-1917.

Northampton County, Virginia, Birth Records 1912-1917.

Northampton County, Virginia, Medical Register.

Northampton County, Virginia, Will Books.

Accomack County, Virginia, Deed Books.

Accomack County, Virginia, Death Records 1853-1896.

Accomack County, Virginia, Birth Records 1853-1896.

Accomack County, Virginia, Will Books.

Federal Census Records

Census for Northampton County, Virginia, 1850-1930.

Census for Accomack County, Virginia, 1850-1930.

Freedmen Bureau Records.

Interviews

George T. Allen

Elizabeth Ames

*George Ayres

Elizabeth Bagwell

Kevin Bagwell

Mary Bagwell

Anna Bailey

Stevie Bailey

Henry Baker

Miles Barnes

Dorothy Bell

*Frances P. Bibbins

George L. Bibbins

*Laura Bibbins

*Lillie Bibbins

*Paul E. Bibbins

James Edward Braxton

Calvin Brickhouse

Alice Brinkley Brown

Laura Chapman

Juanita Coleman

John R. Collin, Jr.

Mirtie Collins

William Collins

Samuel Cooper

Matthew Cornish

James Edward Davis

Conway Downing

Aparo Edwards

Regina Finney

Catherine Kates Fisher

George Floyd

Inez Jones Floyd

Audred L. Finney

Levolia Fletcher

*Jean Burris Fox

Angelo Francis

Hattie Francis

*James Edward Francis

*Jean Whirles Francis

*Lynwood Francis

James Garrison

Alston Joynes Godwin

Juanite Brickhouse Godwin

Thomas G. Godwin

LaRue Holden

Brenda Holden

Ronnie Holden

Thomas Hollis

Marie C. Humbles

Irving Jarvis

Gloria Kates Johnson

Jack Johnson

George Jordan

Oliver Joynes

James A. Kellam

Thomas Kellam

Bessie Kilgo

Lucille Upshur Kornegay

Ranita Major

Alvin Mapp

Naomi Massenberg

Phyllis Mears

David Mitchell

Mabel Mitchell

Eunice Fisher Morris

*Isaiah Nottingham

John W. Nottingham

Mable Owens

*Irene Patterson

*Viola Poole

Jesse Poulson

Jesse Poulson, Jr.

Jeanette Sample

Marion Sample

Kevin Savage

Mary Savage

Rozelma Hunt Savage

*Sallie Seaton

Sam Seymour

Charles Smith

*Lucy Bailey Smith

Denard Spady

Greta Gunter Taylor

George Townsend

Rudolph Tull

Eddie Warren

Linwood Washington

Edgar Wharton

Bessie White

Dorothy Riley White

Brenda Sample Williams

Ida Jones Williams

Vernice Willis

Marvin Wilson

*Henry A. Wise

Ruth Rogers Wise

*deceased

Index

A

ABBOTT
  John E. 92
ACCOMACK COUNTY COLORED HIGH SCHOOL
    ASSOCIATION 94
ACCOMACK COUNTY SCHOOL BOARD 84
ACCOMACK ELEMENTARY SCHOOL 82
ADAMS
  Howard H. 75, 88
  Reverend J. K. 35
ADAMS UNITED METHODIST CHURCH 35
ADDISON
  Addie 68
  Henry 4
AFRICAN BAPTIST CHURCH 37, 43, 71, 101
ALLEN
  Daisy 82
  DeWitt 82
  James 40
  James C. 75
  James H. 65
ALLEN SCHOOL 82
AMERICAN BAPTIST HOME MISSION 64
AMERICAN MISSIONARY ASSOCIATION 82, 96
AMERICAN MISSIONARY SOCIETY 38
AMES
  Alexander 56
  Alfred 5
  Allen T. 5
  George 76
  Jesse 4
  John W. 5
  Richard W. 42
  Smith 76
  Susan 42
AMES FUNERAL HOME 5
ANDERSON
  John M. 83
ANDREWS
  William W. 36
ANNIS
  Emma 60
  George 60
ARMSTRONG
  Samuel Chapman 40, 95

ARMSTRONG SCHOOL 40, 80, 95
ASHBY
  John 91
ATLANTIC SCHOOL BOARD 92
AYRES
  Henny 61
  John "Will" 31
AYRES METHODIST CHURCH 35

B

BAGWELL
  Charles 95
  Nathaniel 65
BAILEY
  Moses 28
  William H. 94
BAKER
  Henry 36
  Samuel 39
BANKS
  Arthur 5
  J. F. 93
  William 5
BANNISTER
  Eugene 16
BAPTIST YOUNG PEOPLE'S UNION 71
BARCLAY
  Reverend 45
BAYLARK
  Reverend Carl 42
BAYLIE
  William 65
BEACH
  Cliff 8
BECKET, BECKETT
  Albert 19
  Charles C. 76
BELL
  Clem 76
  Ellen 61
  Samuel L. 78
BELOTE
  Laban 85
BETHANY ELEMENTARY SCHOOL 83
BETHANY METHODIST EPISCOPAL CHURCH 83
BETHEL A. M. E. CHURCH
    34, 37, 39, 40, 73, 88
BEVANS
  Severn, Sr. 63

129

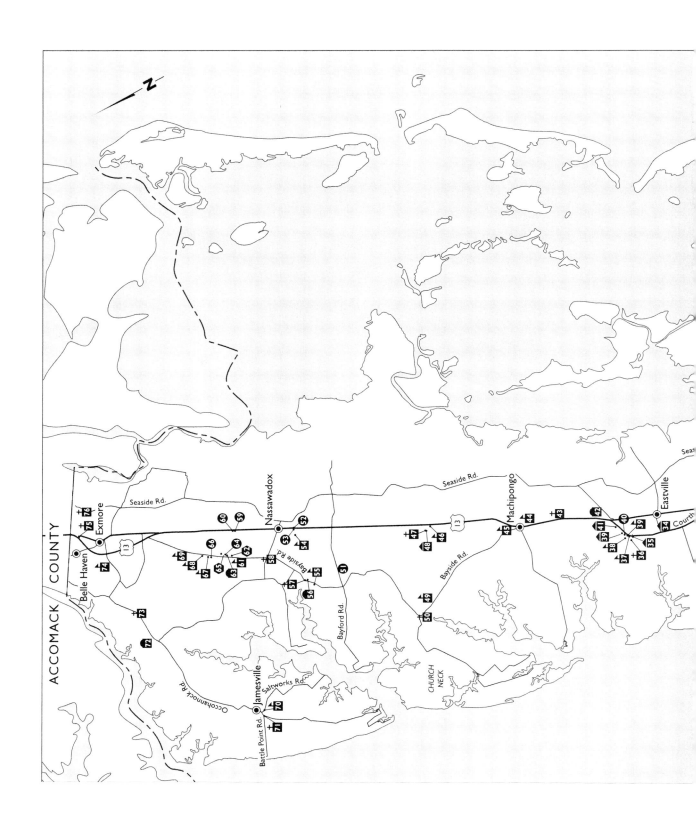

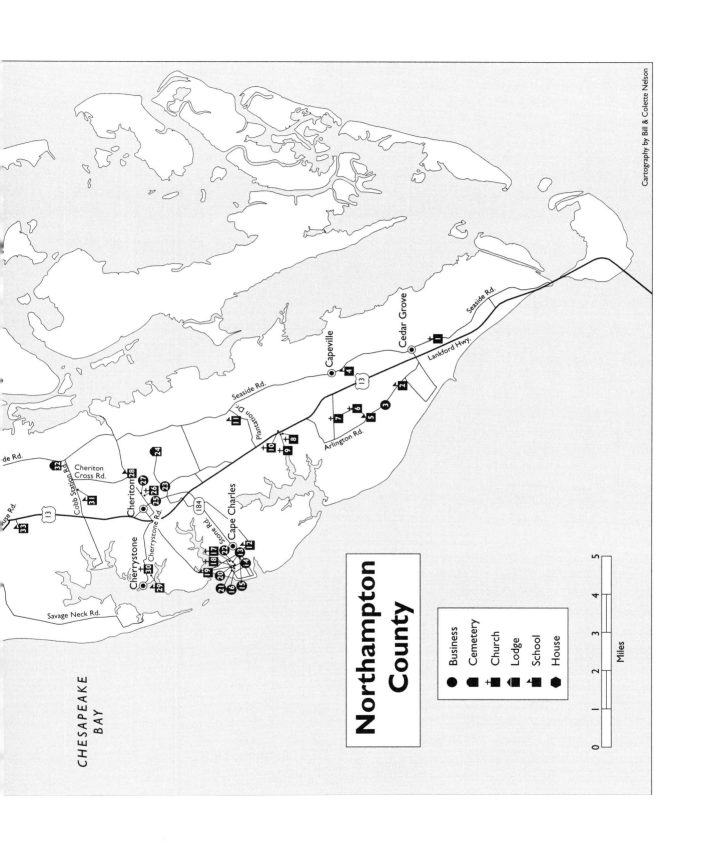

CHESAPEAKE
BAY

Savage Neck Rd.

Cherrystone
Cherrystone Rd.

Cobb Station Rd.

Cheriton Cross Rd.
Cheriton

Cape Charles

Stone Rd.

184

13

Arlington Rd.

Plantation Dr.

Seaside Rd.

Capeville

Cedar Grove

Seaside Rd.

Lankford Hwy.

Northampton County

Business	●
Cemetery	
Church	✝
Lodge	
School	
House	⬢

0   1   2   3   4   5
Miles

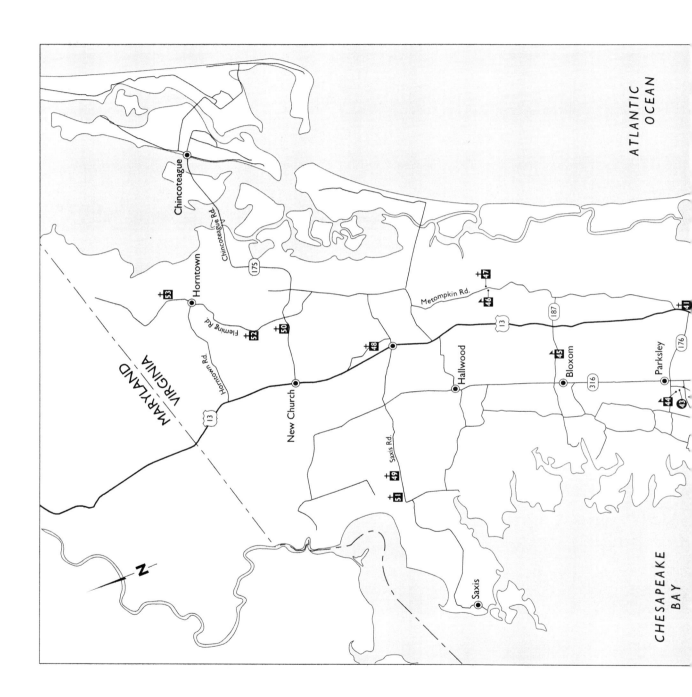

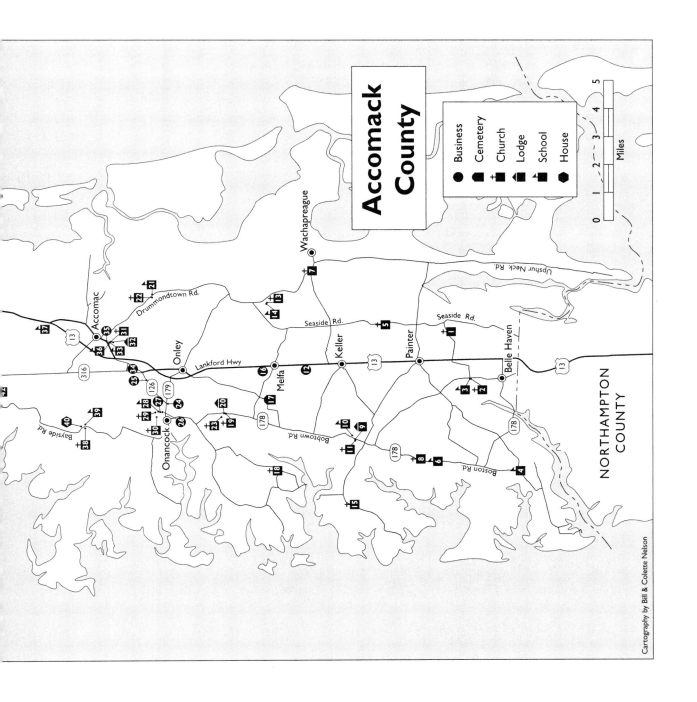

Accomack County

Business ●
Cemetery ⬤
Church ✝
Lodge ▲
School ▰
House ⬢

Miles
0 1 2 3 4 5

Wachapreague

Upshur Neck Rd.

Accomac

Drummondtown Rd.

Seaside Rd.

Onley

Keller

Seaside Rd.

Lankford Hwy

Melfa

Painter

Belle Haven

Bottown Rd.

Onancock

Bayside Rd.

Boston Rd.

NORTHAMPTON
COUNTY

Cartography by Bill & Colette Nelson